MW00776304

♠

Treasury of
Arabic Love

♠

More Treasury of Love
Poems, Quotations & Proverbs

Treasury of African Love
Treasury of Finnish Love
Treasury of French Love*
Treasury of German Love*
Treasury of Hungarian Love*
Treasury of Italian Love*
Treasury of Jewish Love*
Treasury of Polish Love*
Treasury of Roman Love
Treasury of Russian Love*
Treasury of Spanish Love*

*Available as an Audio Book

Hippocrene Books
171 Madison Avenue
New York, NY 10016

♠

Treasury of
Arabic Love

Poems, Quotations & Proverbs
IN ARABIC AND ENGLISH

Edited by Farid Bitar

PROVERBS AND QUOTATIONS
Translated by Ghazi A. Algosaibi

HIPPOCRENE BOOKS
New York

The editor gratefully acknowledges the permission of writers and publishers to reprint the following copyrighted material:

Selections from *Anthology of Modern Arabic Poetry* selected by Mounah A. Khouri and Hamid Algar (University of California Press). "The Procession" is reprinted by kind permission of Philosophical Library. Selections from "Lyrics of Arabia" reprinted by permission of Three Continents Press. Excerpts from 'Ka'b ibn Zuhayr... Banat Su'ad; Mufaddaliyah of Makhabba; al-Sa'di Dhakara r-Rababa; Mufaddaliyah ode of 'Algamath, hal ma 'alimta; from Mu'allaghah of 'Aantarah; and Muffaddaliyah 119 of 'Algamah from REORIENTATIONS edited by Suzanne Stetkevych. Reprinted by kind permission of Indiana University Press. Excerpts from *An Anthology of Modern Arabic Verse*, selected by M.M. Badawi (Oxford University Press, 1970). Reprinted by kind permission of the editor, M.M. Badawi.

* * *

For information, address:
HIPPOCRENE BOOKS, INC.
171 Madison Avenue
New York, NY 10016

Library of Congress Cataloging-in-Publication Data
Treasury of Arabic love poems, quotations, & proverbs / edited by Farid Bitar ; proverbs and quotations translated by Ghazi A. Alghosaibi.
     p. cm.
    English and Arabic (romanized).
    ISBN 0-7818-0395-0
    1. Love poetry, Arabic--Translations into English. 2. Love poetry, Arabic. 3. Quotations, Arabic--Translations into English. 4. Quotations, Arabic. 5. Proverbs, Arabic--Translations into English. 6. Proverbs, Arabic. 7. Love--Quotations, maxims, etc.
I. Bitar, Farid. II. Qusaybī, Ghāzī 'Abd al-Rahmān.
PJ7694.E3T74 1996
892'.710080354--dc20

96-30222
CIP

Printed in the United States of America.

♠

Contents

♠

♠

♠

♠

Arabic Love Poems

♠

Mufaddaliyah 119

taha bika qalbun fi al-hisani tarwbu
    bu`ayda al-shababi `asra hana mashyabu
yukalifuniy layla waqad shatun walyuha
    wa'adat `awaden baynana wkhutubu
muna`amtun mà yustata`u kilāmuha
    `alà babiha min 'an tużāra raqibu
'idha ghaba `anha al-baghlu lam tufshi sirahu
    waturdi 'iyaba al-baghli hiyna ya'uwbu
falà ta`diliy bayni wabayna mughmarn
    saqatki rawaya al-mużni hiyna taswbu
saqaki yamanin dhuw habi wa`aridun
    tarwhu bihi junha al-`ashiyu janwbu
wama 'anta 'am ma dhikruha raba`iyatan
    yukhatu laha min tharmada'a qaliybu
fa'in tas'aluwni bilnisa'i fa'inani
    basirun bi'adwa'i alnisa'i tabiybu
'idha shaba ra'su al-mar'i 'aw qala maluhu
    falaysa lahu min wdahina nasiybu
yuridna thara'a al-mali haythu `alimnahu
    washarkhu al-shababi `indahuna `ajiybu
fada`ha wasali al-hama `anka bijasratn
    kahamika fiha bilradafi khabiybu
'ila al-harithi 'al-wahabi 'a`lamtu naqati
    likalkaliha wal-qusrayayni wajiybu
wanajiyatn 'afna rakyba dulu`iha
    waharikaha tahjurun fada'uwwbu.
        —`Alqamah bnu `Abdah (c. 554 A.D.)

♠

Mufaddaliyah 119 of `Alqamah

A heart turbulent with passion has born you off,
　　Long after youth has passed and the time of old age come.
Thoughts of Laila trouble me though her dwelling is now far,
　　Though there have come between us hostile fates and grave events.
She lives in guarded luxury, all talk with her forbidden;
　　At her door a guard wards off all visitors.
When her husband is away no secret is divulged;
　　Delightful is his homecoming when he returns.
Then do not compare me with an untried youth—
　　May laden rain clouds water you when they let down their loads,
May low-lying Yemeni clouds water you, and clouds spread on the horizon
　　Born on the southwind in the evening when the sun inclines to set.
What good is it to remember her when she is of Rabi'ah's clan
　　And a well is being dug for her in Tharmada'?
If you ask me about womankind, I am indeed
　　Discerning in their ailments, eminently skilled:
Should a man's head hoary or his wealth decrease,
　　He will find no share in their affections;
They seek abundant wealth wherever they know it's found,
　　In youth's first bloom alone they take delight.
So leave her and dispel your cares with a tall mount, bold as your resolve,
　　That even with a second rider keeps up a lively trot,
To al-Harith the Munificent I hastened my she-camel
　　At such a pace her chest and end ribs throb,
A fleet one whose rib-riding hump and hump-front
　　The midday heat and constant journey have consumed.

　　　　　　　　—`Alqamah bnu `Abdah (c. 554 A.D.)
　　　　　　　　Edited by Suzanne Pinckney Stetkevych

11

♠

Mufaddaliyah Dhakara r-Rabāba

Dhakara r-rabāba wa dhikruhā suqmū
    fa sabā wa laysa li man sabā hilmū

wa idhā alamma khayāluhā turifat
    `ayni fa mā'u shu'ūnihā sajmū

ka l-lu'lu'i l-masjūri ughfila fi
    silki n-nizāmi wa khānahu n-nazmū

wa arā lahā dāran bi aghdirati s-
    sidāni lam yadrus lahā rasmū

illā ramādan hāmidan dafa`at
    `anhu r-riyāha khawālidun suhmū

wa baqiyyata n-nu'yi l-ladhi rufi`at
    a`dāduhū fa thawā lahū jidhmū

fa ka'anna mā abqā l-bawārihu wa l-
    amtāru min `arasātihā l-washmū

taqrū bihā l-baqaru l masāriba wa kh
    talatat bihā l-ārāmu wa l-udmū

wa ka'anna atlā'a l-ja'ādhiri wa l-
    ghizlāni hawla rusūmihā l-bahmū

wa laqad tahullu bihā r-rabābu lahā
    salafun yafullu `aduwwahā fakhmū.
                    —*Mukhabbal al-Sa`di (c. 580 A.D.)*

♠

Mufaddal'iyah Dhakara r-Rabāba

He remembered Rabāb. Her memory was sickness.
   He was young again. He didn't know.

When her phantom came round my eye stung
   along the tear lines and began to water,

Pearls slipping
   from a necklace poorly strung.

I make out a dwelling there, hers,
   amid the pools of Sidān, traces unfaded,

Ashes, cold, banked and sheltered from the winds
   by blackened hearthstones

Ruins of a flood-break, stone walls
   around the base, broken in,

As if what the side winds and rains had left
   there on the empty yards were a tattoo.

Doe oryx pasture there, following along toward water,
   white-backs and brown-backs mingling,

The fawns of oryx and gazelle,
   around her tracings, like kids and lambs.

Rabāb might have alighted there, with an advance guard,
   well-armed, to ward off enemies.

                    —*Mukhabbal al-Sa`di (c. 580 A.D.)*
                    Edited by Suzanne Pinckney Stetkevych

♠

Hal mā ʿalimta

Yahmilna utrujjatan nadkhu l-ʿabiri bihā
ka'anna tatyābahā fi l-anfi mashmūmū

ka'anna fa'rata miskin fi mafāriqihā
li l-bāsiti l-muta'ati wahwa mazkūmū

fa l-ʿaynu minni ka'an gharbun tahuttu bihi
dahmā'u hārikuhā bi l-qatbi mahzūmū

qad ʿuriyat zamanan hattā stataffa lahā
kitrun ka hāfati kiri l-qayni mahmūmū

qad adbara l-ʿarru ʿanhā wahya shāmiluhā
min nāsiʿi l-qatirāni s-sirfi tadsimū

tasqi madhāniba qad zālat ʿasifatuhā
hadūruhā min atiyyi l-mā'i matmūmū

min dhidri salmā wa mā dhikri l-awāna bihā
illā s-safāhu wa zannu l-ghaybi tarjimū

sifru l-wishāhayni mil'u d-dirʿi kharʿabatun
ka'annahā rasha'un fi l-bayti malzūmū
            —*Mufaddaliyah ode of ʿAlqamah, (c. 590 A.D.)*

14

♠

Is What You Learned?

They carried an *untrujjah* away. A saffron-scented perfume trailed.
   Before the senses even now her fragrance lingers.

The folds of her hair redolent as musk when the pod is opened.
   Reaching out to touch it even the stuff-nosed is overcome.

Like my weeping eye to a water bag dragged down the well slope
   by a roan-mare camel, withers bound to the saddle stay

For a full season unsaddled, until her hump hardened,
   firm as the rounded side of a smith's bellows.

Cured of the mange and covered
   with a resinous balm, clear and pure,

Spilling water into channels as grain husks part
   from the ripening fruit, the flooded slopes flowing over.

To remember Salma! To recall times spent with her
   is folly, conjecture about the other side, a casting of stones,

Breast sash crossed and falling, gown folds
   at the hip, clinging, soft as a gazelle fawn reared within the yard.
          —From the Mufaddaliyah ode of `Alqamah,
          Edited by Suzanne Pinckney Stetkevych

♠

Al-Mu'allaqah of 'Antarah

idh tastabika bi dhi ghurūbin wādihin
   'adhbin muqabbaluhū ladhidhi l-mat'ami

wa ka'anna fa'rata tājirin bi qasimatin
   sabaqat 'awāridahā ilayka min al-fami

aw rawdatan unufan tadammana nabtahā
   ghaythun qalilu d-dimni laysa bi ma'lami

jādat 'alayhi kullu bikrin hurratin
   fa tarakna kulla qarātin ka d-dirhami

sahhan wa taskāban fa kullu 'ashiyyatin
   yajri 'alayhā l-mā'u lam yatasarrami

wa khalā dh-dhubābu bihā fa laysa bi bārihin
   gharidan ka fi'li sh-shāribi l-mutarannimi

hazijan yahukku dhirā'ahū bi dhirā'ihi
   qadha l-mukibbi 'alà z-zinādi l-ajdhami.
            —'Antarah (c. 590 A.D.)

♠

From the Mu`allaqah of `Antarah

She takes your heart with the flash edge of her smile,
   her mouth sweet to the kiss, sweet to the taste,

As if a draft of musk from a spiceman's pouch
   announced to wet gleam of her inner teeth,

Or an untouched meadow, bloom and grass
   Sheltered in rain, untrodden, dung free, hidden.

Over it the white, first clouds of spring
   pour down, leaving small pools like silver dirhams,

Pouring and bursting, evening on evening
   gushing over it in an endless stream.

The fly has it all to himself, and is not about to leave,
   droning softly, like a wine drinker humming a tune,

Then buzzing elbow on elbow, like a one-armed man
   kindling a fire, bent down over the flint.
               —`Antarah (c. 590 A.D.)
               Edited by Suzanne Pinckney Stetkevych

♠

Bānat Suʿād

bānat suʿādu fa qalbi l-yawma matbūlu
mutayyamun ithrahā lam yuzja makbūlū

wamā suʿādu ghadāta l-bayni idh rahalu
illā aghannu ghadīdu t-tarfi makhūlū

tajlū ʿawārida dhi zalmin idhā ibtasmat
kaʾannahū munhalun bi r-rāhi maʿlūlū

shujjat bi dhi shabamin min māʾi mahniyyatin
sāfin bi abtaha adhā wahwa mashmūlū

tajlū r-riyāhu l-qadhā ʿanhū wa afratahu
min sawbi sāwbi sāriyatin bidun yaʿālilū

ya wayhahā khullatan law annahā sadaqat
ma waʿadat aw law anna n-nasha maqbūlū

lakinnahā khullatun qad sita min damihā
fajʿun wa walʿun wa ikhlāfun wa tabdilū

famā tadūmu ʿalà hālin takūnu bihā
fa mā talawwanu fi athwābihā l-ghūlū

wamā tamassaku bi l-wasli l-ladhi żaʿamat
illā kamā tumsiku l-māʾa l-gharābilū

kanat mawaʿidu ʿurqwbi laha mathalan
wama mawaʿiduha ʾila al-ʿabatilu

ʾarju wāmalu ʾan yaʿjalna fi ʾabadn
wama lahuna tawala al-dahri taʿjiylu

18

♠

Banat Su`ad

Su'ad has departed and today my heart is sick,
    A slave to her traces, unransomed and enchained.

On the morning of departure when her tribe set out
    Su'ad was but a bleating antelope with languid gaze and kohl-lined eye.

When she smiles she flashes side teeth wet
    As if with a first draught of wine or with a second,

Mixed with cool water from wadi's bend, in a pebbled streambed limpid
    And sparkling in the noontime sun, chilled by the northwind,

Cleansed by the winds of all dirt and dust,
    And by white cumuli left overflowing with a night cloud's rain.

Alas! What a mistress, had she been true to what she promised,
    Had true advice not gone unheeded.

But she is a mistress in whose blood are mixed
    Calamity, mendacity, inconstancy and perfidy.

She never stays the same but is as mutable
    as the *ghul* in her garb ever-changing.

Nor does she hold fast love's bond, once she has claimed it,
    Except as sieves hold water.

The false promises of `Urqub were her model,
    Her promises were nothing except empty prattle.

Don't be deceived by the desires she aroused, the promises she made,
    For hopes and dreams are a delusion.

falā yaghuranaka mà mañat wama waʿadat
   'ina al-'amani wal-'ahlama tadlielu

'amsat suʿadu bi'ardn lā yubalighuha
   'ilà al-ʿitaqu al-najiyatu al-marasilu

walan yubalighaha 'ilà ʿudhafiratun
   fiha ʿalà al-'ayni 'irqalun watabghilu

min kulu nadākhati al-dhifra 'idha ʿariqat
   ʿurdatuha tamisu al-'aʿlami majhuwlu
                —Kaʿb ibn Zuhayr (c. 609 A.D.)

Su'ad alit at nightfall in a land unreachable
   But by the best of the she-camels of noble breed and easy pace.

Never to be reached but by a she-camel huge and robust
   That despite fatigue sustains her amble and her trot,

Sweat gushing from the glands behind her ears,
   Eager for the nameless road, its waymarkers effaced.
                    —*Ka`b ibn Zuhayr (c. 609 A.D.)*
                    Edited by Suzanne Pinckney Stetkevych

♠

From the Diwan of `Umar ibn Abi Rabi`a

shaqa qalbi manzilun dathrā,
 halafa l-'arwāha walmatarā
shama'lan tudhri, idha la`ibat
 `āsifan 'dhyaluha l-shajarā
llati qālāt lijaratiha:
 wayha qalbi, mà daha `umarā?
fima 'amsā là yukalimuna?
 wa'idha nataqtuhu basarā
'abihi `utbā fa'u`tibuhu,
 'am bihi sabrun faqad sabarā
'am hadythun ja'ahu kadhibun
 'am bihi hajrun, faqad hajarā

'am liqwlin qalahu kashihun,
 kādhibun, ya laytahu qubirā!
law `alimna mà yusarru bihū,
 mà ta`imna l-barida l-khasirā
wa'rā shawqi sayaqtuluni
 wahabiba l-nafsi 'in hajarā
'inna nawmi mà yulā'imuni,
 'ajlahu, ya 'ukhti, 'in dhukirā
fa'ajābat fi mulātafatin
 'asra`at fiha laha l-hawarā
'inani 'in lam 'amut `ajalan,
 'artaji 'in rāha, 'aw bakarā
fa'idha mà raha, fastalimi,
 'in dana fi tawfihi, l-hajarā.
   — `Umar ibn Abi Rabi`a (644-711 A.D.)

♠

From the Diwan of 'Umar ibn Abi Rabi'a

The ruined camp stirs my heart
  Pledged to the winds and showers
Scattered northward when tops
  Of trees whirl in the storms
For her who said to her maids:
  Alas my heart is 'Umar prudent?
Why does he not speak at eve?
  And when I spoke to him he frowned
If he is content I am content
  Or if he is patient then patient
Or a lying tale comes to him
  Of if he departs then a flight

Or a gossip says words to him
  Falsehoods O would he were dead!
If we knew what pleased him
  We would not feel the cold chill
I know my love will kill me
  And the lover's soul if he flees
My sleep does not last due to
  Him, O sister, if he is thought of
She answered with tenderness
  Hastening to reply to her thus:
If I don't die at once I
  Hope he comes at eve or morning
When he comes at eve he greets
  As he nears in circling the stone.
                —'Umar ibn Abi Rabi'a (644-711 A.D.)
                  Translated by Arthur Wormhoudt

♠

Ila 'Aisha

li`à'ishahta 'ibnahti l-tayami `indi
    haman fi l-qalbi, mà yur`ā hamaha
yudhakiruni 'ibnahta l-tayami zabyun
    yaruwdu birawdatin sahlin rubaha
faqultu lahu, wakada yurā`u qalbi:
    falam 'arà qata kalyawmi 'ishtibaha
siwā hamshin bisaqika mustabiynin,
    wa'nna shawāka lam yushbih shawaha

wa'annaka `ātlun, `ārin, walaysat
    bi`āriyatin, wala `utulin yadaha
wa'annaka ghayru 'afra`a, wahiya tudli
    `alà l-matnayni 'ashama qad kasaha
walaw qa`adat,walam takluf buwddin,
    siwa mà qad kalifitu bihi, kafaha
'azalu, 'idha 'ukalamaha, ka'anni
    'aklamu hayatan ghalibat ruqaha
tabitu 'ilaya ba`da l-nawmi tasri,
    waqad 'amsaytu là 'akhsha surahā.
              —`Umar ibn Abi Rabi`a (644-711 A.D.)

♠

To `Aisha

To `Aisha daughter of Taimi: I have
   A fever in the heart whose heat I fear not
A gazelle reminds me of Taimi's daughter
   As he grazes smooth meadows among the hills
I said to him and he nearly pleased
   My heart: I have not seen the like of today
But for the thinness of your legs that show
   And that your fingers are not as her fingers

And you are unadorned, stripped, and she
   Is not so, nor is her hand without jewels
And you have not long hair and she shows
   Down her back black tresses that cover her
And if she sits and offers not her love
   Except for what I offer her it is enough
Always it seems to me as I speak to her
   I speak to a serpent whose magic overpowers
She comes to me at night after sleep
   I greet her, not fearing her night journey.
            —*`Umar ibn Abi Rabi`a (644-711 A.D.)*
            Translated by Arthur Wormhoudt

♠

Ila Al-Jamielah

qul llmalihati: qad 'ablatni l-dhikaru,
    faddam`u, kula sabahin, fidki yabtadiru
falayta qalbi, wafihi min ta`alqikum
    mà laysa `indi `idlun walā khataru
'afaqa, idh bakhilat hindun, wama badhalat
    mà kuntu āmuluhu minha wa'antaziru
waqad hadhirtu l-nawah fi qurbi dārihumu,
    fa`ila sabri, walam yanfa`iya l-hadharu
qad qultu, idh lam takun llqalbi nāhiyatun
    `anha tusali, walà llqalbi mużdajaru:

ya laytani mittu, idh lam 'alqa man kalafi
    mufarrihan, washāni nahwaha l-nnazaru
washāqani mawqifun bilmarwatayni laha,
    walshawqu yuhadithuhu ll`ashiqi l-fikaru
waqawluha lifatatin ghayri fāhishatin:
    'arā'ihun mumsiyan, 'am bakirun `umaru?
allahu jarun lahu 'ima 'aqama bina,
    wafi l-rahili 'idha mà damahu l-safaru
faji'tu 'amshi walam yughfi al-'awlà samruw,
    wasahibi hinduwaniyun bihi 'uthuru
flam yaru`aha, waqad naddat majasidaha,
    'ilà sawādun, warā'a l-bayti, yastatiru
falatmat wajhaha, wastanbahat ma`aha
    bayda'u ānisatun, min sha'niha l-hafaru.
            —`Umar ibn Abi Rabi`a (644-711 A.D.)

♠

To the Beauty

Say to the beauty: Memory wastes
    And tears for you each morn hurry
Would my heart with your love in it
    Had no such thing or thought within
It sobbed when Hind was stingy and
    Gave not what I hoped and expected
I feared distance near their camp
    As patience tired and caution failed
I said when denial came not to the heart
    To console for her nor urging to the mind:

Would I were dead for I do not find
    One I love in joy as vision turns to her
Standing at the two Marwas stirs me
    Passion is thought created in a lover
Her word to the girl was not stingy:
    Does `Umar come at evening or morning?
Allah aid him in his stay with us
    And on a trip as traveling takes him
I came on foot and the night talkers
    Watched but my Indian friend was tempered
It didn't scare her as she undressed
    Only the dark back of the tent veiled
She touched her face as a bright
    Friend awakened to her, shy on her behalf.
                    —`Umar ibn Abi Rabi`a (644-711 A.D.)
                    Translated by Arthur Wormhoudt

♠

Al-Qalb Al-Mu'thab

shaqa qalbi tadhakkuru l-'ahbabi,
  wa`taratni nawa'ibu l-`atrabi

yā khalilayya, fa`lama 'anna qalbi
  mustahāmun birabbati l-mihrābi

`uliqa l-qalbu min qurayshin thaqālan,
  dhata dalin, naqiyata l-'athwabi

rabatan llnisai fi bayti malakin,
  jadduha hata dhirwahta l-'ahsābi

shaffa `anha muraqaqun janadiyun,
  fahiya kalshamsi min khilala l-sahabi

fatarā'at, hatta 'idha junna qalbi,
  satartaha walā'idun bithiyabi

qultu, lamma darabna bilsatri dwni:
  laysa hadha li`ashiqn bithawabi

fa'jabat mina l-qitayni fatātun,
  dhātu dalin, raqiqatun bi`itabi:

'arsili nahwahtu l-walidataha tas`ā,
  qad fa`alna rida 'abi l-khattabi

là tuti` fi qati`ahti 'ibnati bishrin
  majida l-khaymi tāhira l-'athwabi

fa'itaqi dha l-jalali, ya 'ummu `amruw,
  wahkumi fi 'asirukum bilsawabi.
        —`Umar ibn Abi Rabi`a (644-711 A.D.)

♠

The Suffering Heart

My heart suffers thinking of a lover
    And misfortunes of passion overwhelm me

O my two friends, know that my heart
    Is infatuated with the mihrab mistress

The heart is bound to Quraish gravity
    With good manners and spotless garments

Mistress of women in the king's house
    Her ancestors dwelt on peaks of respect.

The fine janadi is light on her
    She is like the sun seen through clouds

She appears, then my heart faints
    Youthfulness veils her in the clothing

I said as they put a veil before me:
    This is not clothing for those who love

A servant maiden replied
    With good manners and gentle reproof:

Send me to the lady running
    We will do the pleasure of Abu Khattab

Submit not to Bishr's daughter's folk
    Of glorious ancestry, purest garments

Respect that glory O Umm `Amr
    And judge your prisoner with justice.
        —*`Umar ibn Abi Rabi`a (644-711 A.D.)*
        Translated by Arthur Wormhoudt

♠

Mukhtarat I

ya laylati tażdadu nakran
  min huba màn ahbabta bikra
hawra'u 'in nadharat 'ilayka
  saqatka bil`aynayn khamra
waka'ana raj`u hadithuha
  qita`u al-riyad kusiena żahra
waka'ana tahta lisanaha
  harwtu yanfuthu fihi sihra
watakhalu mà jama`at `alayhi
  thiyabaha dhahaban wa`itra
waka'anaha bardu al-sharabi
  safa wwafaqa minki fitra
jiniyah 'insiyah
  'aw bayna dhaka ajalun 'amra
wakafaki 'ani lam 'uhita
  bishakahti màn ahbabtu khabra
'ilā maqalahtu żā'irin
  natharat liya al-'ahżan nathra
mutakhashi'an taht al-hawah
  `ishran watahtu al-mawti `ishra
                    —*The Poet Bassār (711-782 A.D.)*

30

♠

Mukhtarat I

O my night, you grow ever more hateful, because of love I bear
    towards a maiden with whom I have become enamoured.
A sparkling-eyed maiden is she; if she glances towards you,
    she makes you drunk with wine by those two eyes.
The pattern of her discourse seems like meadow plots
    garbed in flowers,
and as though beneath her tongue,
    Harut sat breathing spells therein.
You might well imagine the body on which she gathers her garments
    to be all gold and scent.
It is as though she were the very coolness of drink itself—
    drink pure and suited to your breaking fast.
Be she a maiden of the jinn, a human girl,
    or somewhat between, she is a most splendid thing.
It is enough to say that I never heard tell of any complaint
    about the one I love,
Save the cry of one who would visit her:
    'She has scattered sorrows all around for me,
Victim of passion for a ten-day space,
    and of very death for ten.'
        —The Poet Bassār (711-782 A.D.)
        Translated by A.F.L. Beeston

♠

Mukhtarat II

'ayuha al-saqiyan subba sharabi
    wā'isqiyani min riyq bayda' rawd

'ina da'iy al-zama wa'ina dawa'iy
    shurbah min ridab thaghrin barwd

walaha madhk kaghura al-'aqāhi
    wahadyth kalwasha washa al-burwd

nażalat fi al-sawad min habahta
    al-qalb wanalat żiyadaht al-mustażyd

thuma qalat nalqaka ba`da layaln
    wal-layali yublina kula jadyd

`indaha al-sabru 'an liqa'i wa`indi
    żufrat ya'kulna qalbu al-hadyd
                 —The Poet Bassār (711-782 A.D.)

♠

Mukhtarat II

You two cupbearers, pour out my drink, and give me a draught
  of the moist lips of a delicate fair maiden;

My sickness is thirst, my remedy
  a drink from a cool moist mouth.

She has a smile like the shining petals of the camomile,
  a speech like embroidery, the embroidery of cloaks.

She has settled in the inmost recesses of my heart's core,
  and has won even more than that, like one importunate.

Then she said, `We will meet you some nights hence':
  but the passage of nights will wear out every new thing.

She can rest content without meeting me:
  but my lot is sighs which eat away a heart of iron.
          —*The Poet Bassār (711-782 A.D.)*
          Translated by A.F.L. Beeston

♠

Mukhtarat III

ya sahabaya al-`ashiyahta 'ihtasiba
   jada al-hawah bilfata wma la`iba
wallahi wallahi ma 'anamu wala
   'amluku `ayni dumw`aha taraba
'abqa lana al-dahru man tadhkuru man
   qad kana jāran fabana waghtaraba
lillahi dam`iy 'alā 'ukalimhu
   yawma ghadan fi al-salāfi munsha`iba
ma kana dhanbi ani shuqitu bihi
   washu'mu `aynin kanat lana sababa
'afraghtu dam`iy 'alà al-habiebu fa'a`jabtu
   rijalan walam 'akun `ajaba
qabli tasabah al-fata wamala bihi
   huba al-ma`àsier `alà 'aw khalba
ma kana hubi Salma warw'yatuha
   'ilà qadha fi madami`y nashba
'urydu nisyanaha fayudhakirni
   mà bata fi al-jaratayni muktasiba
lillahi Salma 'idha lā tuti`u bina
   al-washi wa'dh lā nuti`u màn `ataba
tadnuw ma`ah al-dhikru kulama nażaht
   hata 'ara shakhsuha wama 'iqtaraba.
               —*The Poet Bassār (711-782 A.D.)*

♠

Mukhtarat III

O my two friends, for this evening be charitable:
  love is a serious thing for a man, and no sport.
By God, by God, I do not sleep,
  and cannot withhold my eye from its tears of sorrow.
Fate has made to endure for us a memory of one
  who was near but is now distant and remote.
How grievous are my tears, that I may not speak to her
  as on the day she departed, wending her way in distant paths.
What was my crime, that I have been tormented by her?
  What unlucky star was for us cause of grief?
I have exhausted my tears over the beloved,
  and have amazed my folk;
yet I am no marvel—man before me has been befooled by passion,
  and carried away by love of girls, whether that love be chaste or deceitful.
My love for Salma and for the sight of her
  has been truly a mote sticking in my tear-ducts:
I desire to forget her, but then am reminded of her
  by the qualities ever present in my two ladies.
How strange is Salma: she cannot endure one who gossips about us,
  while I cannot endure the one who reproaches me for loving her.
In memory she is near, whenever she is absent,
  so that I behold her person though it is not near.
                    —The Poet Bassār (711-782 A.D.)
                    Translated by A.F.L. Beeston

♠

Al-'āshiq

'ini 'ashiqtu, wama bil'ishqi min ba'si!
   mà marra mithla l-hawa, shay'un 'alà ra'si
mà liya wallnasi, kam yalhuwnani safahan
   dini linafsi, wadinu l-nasi llnasi
mà ll'udati, 'idha mà żurtu mālikati,
   ka'anna 'awjuhahum tutlā bi'anqasi
allahu ya'lamu, mà tarki żiyāratakum,
   ilà makhafahta 'a'dā'i wahurrāsi
walaw qadarna 'alà l-'ityāni, ji'tukum
   sa'yan 'alà l-wajhi, 'aw mashyan 'alà l-ra'si
waqad qara'tu kitāban min sahā'ifikum:
   là yarhamu allahu 'ilà rāhima l-nasi!

ma hawa 'ilà lahu sababun
   yabtadi minhu, wayansha'ibu
fatanat qalbi muhajjabatun
   wajhuha bilhusni muntaqibu
khuliyyat walhusna ta'khudhuhu,
   tantaqi minhu watantakhibu
faktasat minhu tarā'ifuhu,
   wastażadat fadla mà tahabu
fahiya, law sayyarat, fihi, laha
   'awdatan, lam yathniha 'arabu
sara jidan mà mażahtu bihi;
   rubba jiddin jarrahu l-la'ibu.
            — *Abu Nuwas al-Hakami (762-814 A.D.)*

36

♠

The Lover

I loved, there's nothing bad in love
   Nothing like love has ever passed my head
Why is it that folk blame me for folly?
   My religion for me, men's religion for them
Why the foes if I visit my queen
   As if their faces were smeared with ink?
Allah knows my leaving your visits
   Is only for fear of my enemies and guards
If we had power to come, I'd come
   Running on the face or walking on the head
I have read the pages of your book
   Allah doesn't pity unless he pities men.

No passion except for him who has
   A reason to begin it and break it off
A veiled one fascinated my heart
   Her face is covered with beauty
It is left, and beauty takes it
   To perfect it and make it choice
She wears it in its rarities
   And increases the bits she gives
She, if you journeyed to her for it,
   Was a woman whose goal had no second
I went in earnest and did not jest
   The game draws many a serious one with it.
               —*Abu Nuwas al-Hakami (762-814 A.D.)*
               Translated by Arthur Wormhoudt

♠

Wajhu Banan

wajhu Bananin ka'annahu qamarun,
    yalwhu fi laylahti l-thalathini
wal-khaddu, min husnihi wabahjatihi
    kataqati l-shawki fi l-rayahini
yabduru min jabiniha nasamun,
    fi l-tyyibi yahki mabawila l-`ayin
wal-famu min diqihi, 'idha 'ibtasamat,
    kannahu qas`atu l-masākin

laha thanayā tahki bibahjatiha
    wahusniha, 'alsuna l-maważien
wahasbuka l-husnu fi dafa'iriha,
    mithlu l-shamarikhi fi l-`arajin
waljidu żaynun liman ta'ammalahu,
    'ashbahu shay'in bijidi tinnyn
wamankibaha fi husni khalqihima,
    fi mithli rummānatayni min tiyn
walbatnu tāwin, tahki latafathu
    mà dammanuhu kutba l-ddawawyn
walssāqu barrāqatun khalākhiluha,
    ka'nnaha mihraku al-'atātyn

taftinu man rāmaha bilahzatiha,
    ka'nnaha lahzatu l-majaniyn
wa'ahsanu l-nasi mihjaran 'anqan,
    'ashbahu shay'in bimahjari l-nuwn
wa'aqrabu l-nasi fi l-khuta khafaran,
    khutwatuha min nasa 'ilà l-siyn
wulidi min 'usratin mubarakatn,
    là `ayba fiha, min al-shayatyn.
        — *Abu Nuwas al-Hasan al-Hakami (762-814 A.D.)*

♣

Banan's Face

Banan's face is like a moon
    Shining on a month's third night
A cheek in its beauty and glow
    Like a rose bouquet with its thorns
An air comes from her forehead
    Telling of the wild cow's sweet urine
A mouth when it smiles narrowly
    Is like a food tray set for the poor.

Her teeth tell of her brilliance
    And her beauty like balanced tongues
Beauty enough in her braids
    Like date clusters on their stalks
A fine neck for one who sees it
    Similar to the neck of the dragon
Her shoulders in their good shape
    Are like pomegranates among the figs
And belly folds whose softness tell
    Of what they conceal in doctors' books
Legs on whose softness are anklets
    As if they were pokers to stir a furnace.

She enchants one who looks at her
    with a glance whose look is criminal
The finest eye sockets among men
    Something like the whale's eye sockets
Nearest of humans to a snake's glide
    Its step is from Nasa all the way to China
You were born from a blessed clan
    No stain was in it...from the Satans.
                    —*Abu Nuwas al-Hasan al-Hakami (762-814 A.D.)*
                    Translated by Arthur Wormhoudt

♠

Hāmilu l-hawa

hāmilu l-hawa ta`ibu,
    yastakhiffuhu al-ttarabu
'in bakā yuhaqqu lahu,
    laysa mà bihi la`ibu
tadhakiena lāhiyatan,
    walmuhibbu yantahibu
ta`jabiyna min saqami
    sihhati hiya l-`ajabu
kulama 'intafa sababun
    minki, ja'ani sababu

salitu min hubbiha narayni: wāhdatan
    fi wajnatayha, wa'ukhra bayna 'ahsha'i
waqad hamaytu lisani 'an 'abina bihi,
    fama yu`abbiru `anni ghayra 'iymā'i
ya wayha 'ahliya 'ablā bayna 'a`yunihum,
    `alà l-firashi, wama yadruwna mà dā'i
law kana żuhduki fi l-dunyā każuhdiki fi
    hubbi, mashayti bila shakin `alà l-mā'i.
        —Abu Nuwas al-Hasan al-Hakami (762-814 A.D.)

♠

The Bearer of Love

The bearer of love tires
   And passion belittles him
If he wept it was due him
   His trouble was no joke to him
You laughed kindly
   But the beloved lamented
You wondered at my ills
   But my health was the wonder
Each time a bond broke
   Through you a new bond came.

I burn in two fires of her love, one
   Is on her cheeks, the other in my belly
I hold my tongue lest I make it known
   And nothing but my gesture interprets for me
O my folk, I was away before their eyes
   On my bed and they do not know what ails me
If your worldly rigor were as your rigor
   Toward my love you'd walk, no doubt, on water.
         —*Abu Nuwas al-Hasan al-Hakami (762-814 A.D.)*
         Translated by Arthur Wormhoudt

♠

Yukhatib Fw'aduhu

'aqsr fw'adi fama l-dhikra binafi`ah
    walā bishafi`ah fi radi ma kana

salā l-fw'adu l-ladhi shatarathu żamna
    hamala l-sabbabah fa'ukhfuq wahduka l-'āna

ma kana darka 'idh `alaqat shamsu duha
    law 'idkarat dahya l-`ishqu 'ahyana

halā 'akhadhtu lihadha l-yawmu 'ahbathu
    min qabli 'an tusbih l-ashwaqa ashjana

lahafi `alayka qadaytu l-`umra muqtahiman
    fi l-wasli naran wafi l-hijarana mirana.
                    — 'Ismaiel Sabri (1854-1923)

♠

Conversing His Heart

I shorten my heart and remembrance is not useful
    and doesn't advocate in returning what was

Ask the heart that time has separated
    he carried love ardently so beat now alone

What was your hurt if you hanged the sun of dawn
    if you devastated the victims of love sometimes

Would you have taken for this day that you fear
    from before the yearnings became griefs

I lament, for you have spent your lifetime storming
    in connection of fire and in departing fires.
               — *'Ismaiel Sabri (1854-1923)*
               Translated by Farid Bitar

♠

Khada`uwha

khada`uwha biqawlihum hasna'u
walghawani yaghurruhna l-thana'u

'in ra'atni tamilu `anni ka'an lam
taku bayni wabaynaha 'ashya'u!

nazrah fa'ibtisamatun fasalamun
fakalamun famaw`idun faliqā'u

fafirāqun yakwnu fihi dawā'un
'aw firaqun yakuwnu minhu l-dā'u

yawma kunna walā tasal kayfa kunna
natahāda min l-hawah ma nasha'u

wa`alayna min l-`afafi raqiebun
ta`ibat fi mirāsahti l-'ahwa'u

jādhabtani thawbi l-`asi waqalat
'antumu l-nasu 'ayuha l-shu`ara'u

fataquw allaha fi quluwbi l-`adhāra
fal`adhāra quluwbuhunna hawa'u.
— *Ahmad Shawqi (1869-1932)*

♠

They Deceived Her

They deceived her by saying she's a beauty
    And the beautiful women get deceived by praise.

If she sees me, she leans from me as if
    There was nothing between me and her!

A look, a smile, a greeting
    And talking, a date and a meeting

And a farewell in it is a remedy
    Or a farewell from it is a disease

The day we were and don't ask how we were
    Love guides us wherever we wish

And on us from the righteous guardian
    Got tired in the pursuit of passion

The robe of resistance attracted me and said
    You the people, Oh you the poets

Be devout to Allah in the virgins' hearts
    For the virgins, their hearts are passion.
            — Ahmad Shawqi (1869-1932)
            Translated by Farid Bitar

♠

Al-Mawkab I

qalà al-shaykh:
waqul nasiyna fukhar al-fatihyna wama
   yansah al-majanienu hata yaghmuru al-ghamru
qad kana fi qalbi dhi al-qarnayna majaratun
   wafi hashashahu qaiesn haykalun waqaru
fafi 'intisaratu hadha ghulbatun khafiyat
   wafi 'inkisarat hadha al-fawżu wal-zifru
wal-hubu fi al-rwhu la fi al-jimu na`rifuhu
   kalkhamr llwahi la llkasri yan`asru

qala al-fatah:
laysah fi al-ghabat dhikrun
   ghayra dhikru al-`ashiqien
fal'ula saduw wamaduw
   wataghuw bil`alamien
`ashahu mithla hurwf
   fi asāmiy al-mujrimien
fālhawa al-fadah yad`ah
   `indanah al-fath al-mubien
—Gibran Khalil Gibran (1883-1931)

♠

Of Love

Sage :
Forgotten is the glory of the intrepid conquistadors,
    But never 'til the end of time will we forget the paramours!
For in Macedonian's heart we picture but slaughter-house.
    While in the heart of Qais we paint a Rever'd Temple to espouse.
And in the triumph of the first we find an ignoble defeat,
    While in the foiling of the last the victory became complete.
For love lies in the soul alone, not in the body, and like wine
    Should stimulate our better self to welcome gifts of Love Divine.

Youth:
In the forest there is mention
    But of those who madly love;
As to Kings who ruled and lorded,
    And oppress'd from thrones above,
They are but as faded letters
    In the pages of their crime;
Raging passion in its season
    Through the forest reigns sublime.
        —Gibran Khalil Gibran (1883-1931)
        Translated by George Kheirallah

♠

Al-Mawkab II

qala al-shaykh:
fa'in laqaytu muhiban ha'iman kalfan
   fi junw`ihi shab`un wafi wardihu al-sadru
walnasu qaluw huwa al-majnuwn madha `asah
   yabghi min al-hub 'aw yarju fayastaberu
'afi hawa tilka yastadmi mahajirahu
   walaysah fi tilka ma yahluw wayu`tabaru
faqul hum 'ilayhumu matuw qablah ma wulidw
   aniy daruw kinata man yahya wama 'ikhtabaruw

qala al-Fatah:
laysa fi l-ghabati `adhlun
   là walā fiha l-raqieb
fa'idha l-ghuzlān junnat
   idh tarah wajhu l-maghieb
là yaqwl l-nisru wahan
   'inna dha shay'un `ajieb
'inama l-`aqil yud`a
   `indana l-'amru l-gharieb
            —*Gibran Khalil Gibran (1883-1931)*

♠

Of Love

Sage :
Now should you meet a lover lost, bewildered, yet avoiding guide,
    Disdaining though he thirsts to drink, in his own hunger satisfied;
Hear people say, "This youth bewitched what seek he from love so great?
What hope has he to patiently await his Kismet and his Fate?
Why waste his bloodstained tears for one
    Who lacks all beauty and respect?"
Say of them all, they are stillborn,
    Know naught of life, nor can reflect.

Youth:
In the woods no blame attaches
    To lover's tryst, nor watchers spy;
When a gazelle, ranging swiftly,
    Greets its lovemate with a cry,
Eagles never display wonder,
    Or say,"'Tis marvel of the ages."
For in nature we the children
    Only hold the sane as strange.
                —*Gibran Khalil Gibran (1883-1931)*
                Translated by George Kheirallah

Al-Mahabah

hina'dh qalat lahu al-mutrah: hata lana khutabah fi al-mahabah.
farafa'a ra'suhu wanadhar ila al-sh`ab nadhrata
mahabah wahanan. fasmatu jamy`uhum
khashi`yn. faqala lahum biswt `adhiem:
'idha 'asharat al-mahabah 'ilaykum fa'tabi`uha.
wa'in kanat masalikuha sa`bah mutahdirah.
wa'idha damatkum bijanahyha fi'ti'wha.
wa'in jarahakum al-saief al-mustawri bayna rishiha.
wa'idha khatabatkum al-mahabah fasadiqwha.
wa'in `atala sawtuha 'ahlamukum wabadadha kama
taj`al al-riyh al-shamaliyah al-bustan
qa`an safsafan.

li'anahu kama 'ana al-mahabah tukalilakum.
fahiya 'aydan taslubukum.
whama ta`mal `ala numuwkum.
hakadha tu`alimukum watast'sil al-fasid minkum.
wakama tartafi`u 'ila 'a`la shajarah hayatukum
fatu`aniq 'ghsanuha al-latiefah al-murta`isaha
'aman wajhu al-shams.
hakadha tanhadiru 'ila judhuruha al-multasiqah
bilturab watahżuha fi sakienah al-layl.

al-mahabah tadumukum 'ila qalbiha ka'aghmar al-hintah.
watudarisukum 'ala bayadiraha likai tutahira `aryakum.
watugharbilakum likai tuharirukum min kushurukum
watathanukum likai taj`alukum 'anqiya' kathalj.
wata`jinakum bidumu`aha hata talinw.
thuma ta`idakum linariha al-muqadasah.
likai tasyrew hubjan muqadasan yukarabu `alà
ma'idahtu al-rab al-muqadasah.

kulu hadha tasna`ahu al-mahabah bikum likai
tudriku 'asrara qulukikum. fatusbihu
bihadha al-'idraka jużan min qalb al-hayah.

50

♠

Al-Mahabah

Then said Almitra, Speak to us of Love.
    And he raised his head and looked upon
the people, and there fell a stillness upon
them. And with a great voice he said:
    When love beckons to you, follow him,
    Though his ways are hard and steep.
    And when his wings enfold you yield to him,
Though the sword hidden among his
pinions may wound you.
    And when he speaks to you believe in him,
    Though his voice may shatter your dreams
as the north wind lays waste the garden.

    For even as love crowns you
so shall he crucify you.
Even as he is for your growth
so is he for your pruning.
    Even as he ascends to your height and
caresses your tenderest branches
that quiver in the sun,
    So shall he descend to your roots and
shake them in their clinging to the earth.

Like sheaves of corn he gathers you unto himself.
    He threshes you to make you naked.
    He sifts you to free you from your husks.
    He grinds you to whiteness.
    He kneads you until you are pliant;
And then he assigns you to his sacred fire,
that you may become sacred bread for God's sacred feast.

    All these things shall love do unto you
that you may know the secrets of your heart,
and in that knowledge become a fragment of life's heart.

♠

ghayra anakum 'dha khiftum.
waqasartum sa`yukum `alà al-tuma'ninah wal-lidha
fi al-mahabah:
fa'al'jdar bikum 'an tastarew `aryakum watakhrujuw
min baydar al-mahabah 'ila al-`alam
al-ba`iyd haythuma tadhakuwn. walaken laysah kulu duhkikum.
watabkuwn. walaken laysah kulu ma fi ma'ākyhum min al-dumuw`.

l-mahabah là tu`tiy 'ila nafsaha.
walà ta'khudhu 'ila min nafsaha.
al-mahabah là tamluku shaya'an.
wala turiydu 'an yamlukha 'ahad:
li'ana al-mahabah muktafieah bil-mahabah.

'ama 'anta 'idha 'ahbabta fala taqul:
" 'ina Allahu fi qalbiy" bal qul bil-ahrah:
" 'ana fi qalbu allahu".
wala yakhtur laka al-batah anaka tastatiy`u
'an tatasalat `ala masalik al-mahabah-li'ana
al-mahabah. 'in ra'at fiyka 'istihqaqan lin`matiha.
tatasalat hiya `ala masalikak.
wal-mahabah là raghbah laha 'ila fi 'an tukamil nafsaha.
walakin 'idha 'ahbabt, wakana la buda min 'an takuwna laka
raghabat khasah bika, faltakun hadhihi raghabatuku:
'an tadhuwb watakuwn kajadwal mutadafq yashnuf
ādhan al-layl bi'anghamihi.
'an tukhaber al-āalam al-lati fi al-`atf al-mutanahi.
'an yajrahka 'idrakui al-haqiqi lil-mahabah fi hubatu qalbuka,
wa'an tanżuf dima'uka wa'nta radin mughtabt.
'an tanhad `inda al-fajr biqalb mujnah khafuwq, fatuw'adi wajibu al-shukru
multamisan yawma mahabah ākhr.
'an tastariyh `inda al-zahirah watunaji nafsakah
biwajd al-mahabah.
'an ta`wd ila manżilika `inda 'al-masa' shakiran:
fatanam hiyna'dh wal-salah li'jla màn 'hbabt tataradad fi
qalbika wa'unshwdahtu al-hamd wal-thana' murtasimah `ala shafatayk.
—*Gibran Khalil Gibran (1883-1931)*

52

♠

But if in your fear you should seek only
love's peace and love's pleasure,
    Then it is better for you that you cover
your nakedness and pass out of love's threshing-floor,
    Into the seasonless world where you
shall laugh, but not all of your laughter,
and weep, but not all of your tears.

    Love gives naught but itself and takes
naught but from itself.
    Love possesses not nor would it be possessed;
    For love is sufficient unto love.

    When you love you should not say,
"God is in my heart," but rather, "I am
in the heart of God."
    And think not you can direct the course
of love, for love, if it finds you worthy,
directs your course.
    Love has no other desire but to fulfill itself.
    But if you love and must needs have
desire, let these be your desires:
    To melt and be like a running brook
that sings its melody to the night.
    To know the pain of too much tenderness.
    To be wounded by your own understanding of love;
    And to bleed willingly and joyfully.
    To wake at dawn with winged heart
and give thanks for another day of loving;
    To rest at the noon hour and meditate love's ecstasy;
    To return home at eventide with gratitude;
And then sleep with a prayer for the
beloved in your heart and song of praise upon your lips.
                —*Gibran Khalil Gibran (1883-1931)*
                    Translated by Al-Erismendit Antonios Bashier

♠

Al-Wardah Al-Dhabilah

'arjun ka'anfasi l-habibah
  hina tudni minka fāha
waghalā'ilun bata l-ghamamu
  yajuwdaha hata rawaha
dhabilat wa'khlaqa husnuha
  ya layta shi`ri ma dahaha
rawaytuha bimadami`i
  law kana yhayyha hayaha
wadammtuha dama l-habibu
  `asah ya'wdu laha sibaha
ważafartu 'alāa żawafiri
  tajdi fażadat fi dhuwaha
faramaytuha wbiraghmi
  'anfi 'anani min qad ramaha
walaw 'istata`tu hanaytu 'ad
  lā`i `ala dhawi sanaha
waja'altu sadri kabruha
  waja`altu 'ahsha'i tharaha.

      —'Ibrahim `Abd al-Qadir al-Mazini
      (1890-1949)

♠

The Wilted Rose

Fragrance like your lover's breaths
   when her mouth comes near you.
And dried up land, the clouds passed by
   with heavy rains until he quenched her thirst.
It wilted and her beauty was more natural
   would God! If only my poetry didn't make her clever.
I watered her with my tears—
   if possible to make her live, it would have
And I embraced her in the lover's embrace
   perhaps her youth will return to her.
And I moaned so perhaps my moaning
   will help, but it wilted even more
And I threw her against my
   will, I am the one that threw her.
And if I could, I would bend
   my ribs on her wilted splendor
And I would make my chest her grave
   and I would make my intestines her soil.
        —'Ibrahim `Abd al-Qadir al-Mazini (1890-1949)
        Translated by Farid Bitar

Al-Nayi Al-Muhtariq

kam maratin ya habibi
   wal-layli yaghsha l-baraya
'ahimu whdi wama fi l-zalāmi
   shaki suwaya
'asayara l-dam`u lahnan
   wa'j`al l-sha`ra naya
wahal yulabiy hutamu
   'ash`ltahu bijawaya
al-naru tuwaghlu fihi
   wal-rihu tadhurwu l-baqaya
mà 'at`as l-nayi bayna
   l-muna wabayna l-manaya
yashdw wayasdhw haẓinan
   muraji`an shakwaya
musta`tifan man tawayna
   `alà hawahu l-tawaya
hata yalwhu khayalu
   `ariftahu fi sabaya
yadnuw 'ilaya watadnuw
   min thaghrihi shafataya
'idha bihulmi talasha
   wa'istayqazat `aynaya
waruhta 'asghi wa'asghi
   lam 'alfi 'ilà sadaya
      — `Ibrahim Naji (1898-1953)

♠

The Burning Flute

How many times my love
   as the night covers the earth
I wander alone, and in the dark
   no one complains but me.
I make the tears a tune
   and I make the poetry a flute
And would a wreck responds
   that I inflamed in my ardent love.
Fire stirs in it
   and the wind blows away the rest.
How miserable is the flute between
   destiny and between fates
He sings and sadly sings
   returning my complaints.
Sympathetic from our kept secrets
   on the love of innermost secrets
Until a shadow appears.
   I have known him in my youth
He comes close to me and he comes close
   to the lips of my mouth
And suddenly my dream disappears
   and my eyes wake up
And though I went listening and listening
   I wasn't familiar but with the echo.

                — `Ibrahim Naji (1898-1953)
                Translated by Farid Bitar

♠

Hulmu Al-gharām

lā hubu 'ilā haytha hala walā 'ara
   li ghayra dhalika mawtinan wamaqama
watani 'alā twla l-layali dāruhu
   mahma na'ā wahawaya haythu 'aqama
wal-ardu hina tadumuna ma'hwlatan
   lahazatuha ma`mwratan ayāma
la farqa bayna shamluha wajanwbiha
   fahuma liqalbi yahmilani salama
wahuma li'ahdi hafizani waqalama
   hafiza l-żamanu lmuhjatayni dhimama
wa'idha bakaytu faqad bakaytu makhafatan
   min 'an yakwa gharamuna 'ahlama
walarubama khatara l-nawah fabakaytuhu
   min qabla 'an ya'ti l-bu'adu sijama

               — *'Ibrahim Naji (1898-1953)*

♠

The Dream of Infatuation

No love but wherever held a place and I don't see
    for me other than that a homeland and a location
My homeland all nights long is his home
    as long and as far away he gets, my love is where he stays.
And when inhabited earth embraces us
    its moments are populated daily.
No difference between her north and south
    as they are bearing greeting to my heart
And they are pressing my knowledge and seldom
    time preserves the custody of my heartbloods.
And if I cry, so I cry from the fear
    that our infatuation is just a dream
And maybe the significance of our intention. So I cried out
    from before we shed the tears from our distance.
               — 'Ibrahim Naji (1898-1953)
               Translated by Farid Bitar

♠

'Ughniyaha Ryfiyaha

'idha da'aba al-ma'u zila al-shajar
   waghazalat al-suhub dw'a al-qamar
wradadat al-taier 'anfasuha
   khawafq bayna al-nada wal-żahr
wanahat mutwaqah bilhawa
   tanajy al-hadyl watashkw al-qadar
wamara `ala al-nahr thaghru al-nasiem
   yuqabilu kula shra` `abar
wa'tla'at al-'ard min layliha
   mafatn mukhtalifat al-suwar
hunalika safsafah fi 'al-duja
   ka'ana al-zalam biha ma sha`ar
'akhdhtu makany fi dhiliha
   sharydu 'al-fu'adi ka'ibu 'al-nazar
'amuru bi`ayni khilal 'al-sama'
   wa'atruqu mustaghriqan fi 'al-fikr
'utali` wajhaki taht 'al-nakhiel
   wa'asma` swtuki `inda 'al-nahr
'ila 'an yamilu 'al-duja wahshaty
   watashkw 'al-kàabah miny 'al-dajar
wat`jab min hyraty 'al-ka'nat
   watashfaq miny nujum al-sihr
fa'amdy li'arj` mustashriqan
   liqa'uki fi al-maw`d al-muntadhar.

                —*`Ali Mahmoud T'aha (1902-1949)*

♠

A Rustic Song

When the water caresses the shade of the tree,
   And the clouds court the light of the moon;
And the birds send forth their song
   To re-echo between dew and blossom;
And the ringdove laments her passion,
   cooing to her love and bemoaning her fate;
And the lips of the breeze pass over the Nile,
   Kissing every passing sail;
And the earth brings forth from its night,
   There in its shade I take my place,
With heart distraught and saddened gaze.
   I let my eyes wander through the skies,
My head downcast and sunk in thought.
   Then, I see your face beneath the palm tree,
And by the river I hear your voice,
   Until darkness is tired of my loneliness,
And sadness complains of boredom;
   Until creation wonders at my bewilderment,
And the morningstar
   Takes pity on me;
And I go on my way,
   To search again in hope
For our encounter
   At the longed-for hour.

—`Ali Mahmoud T'aha (1902-1949)*
Translated by Mounah Khouri & Hamid Algar

♠

'Imra'ah Watimthal

hasna', hadhy dumyatun
   manhwtatatun min marmar
tala`at `ala 'adunya
   tulw` al-sakhr al-mustahter
wasarat 'ila haram al-khulwd
   `ala riqab al-'a`sr
`aryanah sukar al-khayal

   bi`aryaha al-mutakabir
'abadan mumti`atun biyanbw`u
   al-saba al-mutafajer
tarnw 'ilyha fi wujum
   al-halim al-mustafsir
wal-tarfu bayna munaqlin
   fi sihriha wamusamer
washah biha, 'ibda` nahitha,
   al-jamal al-`abqary
wamada, wabintu rw'ahu
   lam takbar, walam tataghayar
hasna', ma 'aqsa fajàat
   al-żaman al-'ażwar
'akhsha tamwtu rw'ay 'in
   tataghayary...fatahjary.
            —`Umar 'Abu Rishah (b. 1910)

♠

A Woman and a Statue

O beautiful one!
  behold this statue carved of marble,
Looking down on the world with cynical disdain
  And advancing across the ages
  to the shrine of immortality.
Naked, intoxicating
  the imagination with her arrogant nakedness;
Eternally enjoying
  the gushing spring of youth;
One gazes upon her
  with the wonder of questing dreamer,
And the eyes move across her magic,
  lingering, entranced.
The sculptor's genius made of her
  an adornment to eternal beauty,
Then passed on, and the daughter of his vision
  remained, youthful and unchanging.
O beautiful one!
  How cruel are the sudden blows of crooked fate!
If you change,
I fear that my vision may die
  ...so be turned to stone!

—*'Umar 'Abu Rishah (b. 1910)*
Translated by Mounah Khouri & Hamid Algar

Qasru Al-Habibah

abtaniy, kula laytatun,
laki qasran munawran,
hajran min zumurad,
wamin al-masi ahjuran.
ayu lawnin? samau' `ynayki
'am khudratu al-dhurah?
anà qasriy min kuli mah
sh'ti: kuniy fa-yahdurah.
tay`un, w'uhzy yater
biki tayran, wyaskarah.
khytu du'in yarqy bihi
sawba najmayn ghuran
wathwanin yadfa`anahu,
ghumad al-jafni sumrah.

wa'idhā juẓtuma al-madah,
wamin al-nuru abhara,
anà, 'in anty humti biya,
walsuha hwluna yura,
abtani fi al-nujumi liya
ba`lbaka, wtadmurah!
balighy qubaten biha
yusna`u al-hulmu walkara,
fa'is'ly `an asabi`u
liya, masat dhaka al-tharah,
ẓra`athu, warahabat
kabla ann ẓarti _ aẓhura,
`alahu yaghtadi ilà
qasraki al-huw, m`baran!

waithà ma malaltihi,
wasà wahshatn `ara,
watathakarti arduna
wrubaha, wal'anhurah,

The Palace of My Beloved

I will build for you each night
A palace luminous
With whole blocks of emerald
And diamond stones.
Shall it be sky blue as your eyes,
or green as the hilltops?
It will be made of your wishes:
Be, and the palace too shall be.
Sing softly, and obedient it will take you
And fly aloft like a drunken bird,
And rise on a thread of light,
Seeking two sunken stars;
Driven on by the seconds of time,
Their eyes closed in the discourse of night.

When together you have traversed
The expanse, and the oceans of light,
And reached the dome of heaven
Where sleep and dreams are made,
Ask after those my fingers
Which once touched that soil,
Sowed there flowers of welcome
Before your visit came,
That might one day mark
The way to your fine palace.
Should you tire of the palace,
Of the pain of solitude and grief,
And remember this our earth,
Its hills and streams,

Then whisper and I shall come,
Then world's verdure in my cloak.
With sickness past, ask, O my desire,
That I erect anew the ruin.

♠

fa'hjusiy biya 'uqabil, wafi
burdati al-kawnu akhdara.
tbti, ya matlabi, 'utlubi,
ba`da hadmen, fa-'mura.
wa'qulu:" Imrahi. Imrahi
w'uqtufiy al-shuhaba kalkura,
laki, lilahui, lilhawa,
budala al-kawnu manzaran.
                    —Sa`id Aql (b. 1912)

♠

If you love with a passion
That sheds luster on the dimmest star,
Then will I build myself in the skies
A Baalbek or Palmyra,
And say: "Rejoice, be gay,
Catch each comet like a ball,"
With the world as but a show
For you, your amusement and your whim.

    —Sa`id Aql (b. 1912)
     Translated by Mounah Khouri & Hamid Algar

♠

Samrà'u

Samrà'u, ya hulma al-tufulahtu
watamn`u al-shufatu al-bakhylatu
là taqrubi mini, wazalily
fikratun, leghadi, jamilahtun.

qalbi maliy'un bilfraghi
alhulú, fājatni dukhulahu
'akhsha `alyhi yghasa
bilqubal al-mutayabah al-balylahtu
wayghibu fi al-àfaqï
`abra al-hùdabu min `ayna kahylah!

mà ākhudhu minka al-bahù
wamin ghada'iruka al-jadylah?
dw'àn? fadaytu al-dw'a yulada
tayà taftatikï al-'alylah;
wyqulu lilbasmati thaghruki.
"lwuniy żhra al-jamilah"
fal'ardu ba`dáki ykztun
min hj`ahu al-hulmi al-thqylah
taribat, k'ana sana ibtisamiky
kuwatun al-ámal al-za'iylahtu.

samrà'u, zalily ldhatun
bayna al-ladha'idhu mustahylah;
zalily `alá shafataya shwqahama
wafi jafny dhulāh;
zalily al-ghda al-manshuda
yasbuquna al-mamatu 'ilayhi `iylah.
            —Sa`id Aql (b. 1912)

68

Samrà'u

Samara, O childhood dream,
Impregnable, miserly lips,
Approach me not, remain as
A thought of beauty for my morrow.

My heart is full of a sweet
Void; so enter it not.
I fear it would choke
Beneath your moist, perfumed kisses,
And vanish over the horizon
Through your kohl-anointed lashes.

What has beauty taken
From you and your plaited trees?
Its light? I would gladly die for the light
Born of your languid glance.
Your mouth replies to a smile:
"Go, paint the corpse's flowers."
The earth as you pass is an awakening
From the deep slumber of dream,
Joyous as if your flashing smile
Were some small chink of hope.

Samara, remain one among
The unattainable delights;
The object of my lip's desire
And of my distraught gaze;
That morrow for which we long
And death, stealing forward, grasps.
  —Sa`id Aql (b. 1912)
   Translated by Mounah Khouri & Hamid Algar

♠

Al-Hub fi San Lazar

fi mahatat victoria jalastu wabiyadi maghżal
wakana al-maghżal maghżal 'odysios
`afwan 'itha 'ikhtalafna 'ayuha al-qari'u
faqad ra'aytuhum,ra'aytuhum sukana al-'arjw,
wajalahum mina al-nisa'i 'irtadayna
al-bantalwnat walabisna 'ahthyah min kawtshuk.
'ama nahnu, anta wal-fareed barwfruka wa'na
falana al-maghazl nata`alal biha, wabayna
alkhyt walkhyt narfa` 'ahdabana ila al-'amwaj
fi al-'ufq, la`ala mawj al-'ufq yahmil al-'arjw
wafi al-sabah, `indama yasier mawj al-'ufq mawj
al-shat', nara wajhu al-sa`adah.
jalastu wabiyadi maghzaly fi 'intdhar Penelope
'al-laty là 'a`rifha
wahal atat Penelope ilà rasief numrah 8?
kala, lam ta'ti Penelope ilà rasief numrah 8?
　　　　　　　　—*Lewis `Awad (b. 1915)*

♠

Love at St. Lazare

At Victoria Station, I sat holding a spindle.
It was the spindle of Odysseus.
(Forgive me, reader, for the change involved).
I saw them, I saw them,
the dwellers on the Argosy,
mostly women wearing trousers and rubber shoes.
As for us, that is, you, Alfred Prufrock and myself,
we have spindles with which to while away our time.
Between threads, we raise our eyes to the waves on the horizon,
in the hope that they might be bearing the Argosy,
and in the morning,
when the wave on the horizon becomes the
wave on the shore, we might see the face of happiness.
I sat holding my spindle waiting for the unknown Penelope.
Did Penelope come to platform eight?
No, Penelope did not come to platform eight.

$\qquad$ —*Lewis `Awad (b. 1915)*
$\qquad$ *Translated by Mounah A. Khouri & Hamid Algar*

Lan 'Aby`u Hubuhu

'aya sudfaha
sudfaha kalhulmi hilwah
jama`atna hahuna fi hadhihi al-'ard al-qasyaha
nahnu rwuhan gharyban huna
'alafat ma baynana
rabatu al-fan, waqad tafat bina
fa'idha al-ruwhan ghinwah
sabahat fi lahn (muwajarat) wadunyahu al-ghaniyah
qulta: fi `aynayki `umq,
'anti hilwa
qultaha fi rughbah mahmuwsah al-jaras _
'inahu 'ibn bilady lan 'abiy`u
hubuhu
bikunwż al-ardi
bi-'alanjum żahran
bilqamar
ghayru 'aniy ta`tary qalby nashwah
fama kunna bikhlwah
wabi`ynayka nida'
wabi'a`maqy nashwah
'aya nashwah
'ana 'untha fa'ghtafir lilqalb zahwah
kulama daghdagha hamsuki: fi `aynayki `umq
'anti hulwah
'ana ya sha`r liy fi watany
watany al-ghaliy habibun yantazr
'inahu 'ibn bilady lan 'uday`
qalbuhu
hiynama tatfwu zilal al-hub fi `aynayka
'aw tuwmad da`wah
'ana 'untha, faghtafir lilqalb żahwah
kulama daghdaghahu hamsuka: fi `aynayka `umq
'anti hulwah.
—*Fadwa Tuqān (b. 1917)*

72

I Won't Sell His Love

What chance
Sweet dreamlike chance
Joined us here in this distant land
Here two strange souls we
Were united by the Muse
Who carried us away
Our souls becoming a song
Floating on a Mozart air
In its precious world
You said: How deep your eyes
How sweet you are
You said it with hushed, echoing desire
For we were not alone
And in your eyes an invitation
And in my depths intoxication
What intoxication
I am a women so forgive my heart its vanity
When your murmur caresses it: How deep your eyes
How sweet you are
O poet, in my country, my beloved country
I have a sweetheart waiting
He is my countryman I won't squander
His heart
He is my countryman I won't sell
His love
For the world's treasures
For the shining stars for the moon
Yet intoxication grips my heart
As in your eyes drift love's shadows or invitation glimmers
I am a woman so forgive my heart its vanity
When your murmur caresses it: How deep your eyes
How sweet you are.

                     —Fadwa Tuqān (b. 1917)
                Translated by Mounah Khouri & Hamid Algar

♠

Al-Qasidah 22

'ila 'an 'inżaha al-sitar al-'akhier
kana fi hubuna naqsun
khafiyun 'aliem.
kitaban kuntu laki, wakunti liy kitaban,
w`ala al-rafi 'alfu safar;
w'ukhtan kunti liy, wakuntu laki 'akhan,
wakulu man fi al-kawni 'ikhwanu.
fa'in ghibti wa'in ghibtu
'intafada al-hubu walam ya`takf.
walam nadri ('alam nadri?)
'ann kāna fi hubana naqun
khafiun 'aliem
zanana hubana al-kamal
(zanana 'am ta`amina?)
faq`adna 'indahu, saqama,
walam naltafet 'ila hwuden qareeb
tamahy al-asqamu fihi
wayablughu al-hubu ba`daha al kamal,
hata tara'ah lana al-sitaru al-muqiet.
bila 'arjulen sa`yna,
baty'an żahafna;
hal khashyna al-miyah?
min miyah al-ba`th 'irt`abna.
(ra'dyin kunna, 'am kunna nażwru 'awtanan?)
wafi al-hwdi 'irtamiena,
'irtamiena hata 'irtawana
`indama 'inżaha al-sitaru al-'akhier.
—*Tawfiq Sayigh (1923-1971)*

♠

Poem 22

Until the last veil was cast aside
There was a blemish on our love
Hidden, painful.
I was a book to you, and you to me,
And on the shelf a thousand tomes;
You were a sister to me, and a brother I to you,
And all on earth are brothers.
Should you disappear, or I,
Then Love would tremble, yet not fade away.
We did not know (did we not?)
That there was a blemish on our love,
Hidden, painful.
We supposed our love perfection
(Did we suppose, pretend not to see?)
So indolent we remained, ailing
Heedless of a nearby pool
In which ailments are dissolved
And afterwards love attains perfection;
Until the hateful veil was revealed to us.
Legless we proceeded,
Slowly, slowly we crept
Did we fear the waters?
We were alarmed at the waters of resurrection.
(Were we explorers, or visiting our homelands?)
We plunged into the pool,
We immersed ourselves until we quenched our thirst
When the last veil was cast aside.
                    —*Tawfiq Sayigh (1923-1971)*
                    Translated by Mounah Khouri & Hamid Algar

♠

Al-Qasidah 23

khad`tany, falam 'ubali:
li'naki 'intaqyti
yawma bahathi `an habibin
sadyqi
ahbabtihi, waqablaki ahbabtuhu,
fatalaqa huby whubuky;
waykfiny.
kaná yakfiny
law anāki lam tahdufy
'an takhnuky sadakahati lahu
bihubuki
'an takhnuqi al-sadakahta
watasra`y al-huba:
'an tadhbahy al-fatah
`ala mar'ah 'abyhu,
waba`daha tadhbahyhu.

lam 'ubali:
li'anna hubaki kaná saykhbw
al-yama 'aw ghadan,
fakhaba al-yama
wastarahtu.

ta`antany falam 'aqdi,
waltafatu, fa'dha 'anti al-laty tulhadyn.
w`ala ramsiki khatatu:
"faltamut habibaty, waly`sh sadykiy."
—*Tawfiq Sayigh (1923-1971)*

♠

Poem 23

You deceived me,
yet I minded not
For you chose
That day you sought a lover
My friend.
You loved him,
and I loved him before,
So my love merged with yours;
And I am content.
I would have been content
Had you not designed
To stifle affection
And dash Love against the ground:
To immolate the youth
Before his father's eyes,
And then to slay the father.

I minded not:
For your love would have expired
Tomorrow or today,
And it died today
And I found peace.

You thrust at me, yet I did not die,
I turned and Lo! It is you they are interring.
I inscribed upon your tomb:
"May my beloved die, and my friend live."
        —*Tawfiq Sayigh (1923-1971)*
            Translated by Mounah Khouri & Hamid Algar

♠

Risalatuh hub saghyrah

habibaty,
ladayà shay'un katheir...
akwluhu, ladayà shay'un katheir
min 'ayuna? ya ghaliyaty abtady
wakulu ma fiki... amirun...amir
ya 'anti, ya ja`ylatun 'ahrufy
mima biha, shraniqun lilharyr
hādhy 'aghani... whādha anā
yadumuna hādhà al-kitabu al-saghyer...
ghadan, idha qalabti awraquhu
washtaqa misbahun.. waghna sareerun
wa'khdwdarat min shwquha 'ahrufun
w'awshakat fawasilun 'an tatier...
fala taquly: ya lihatha al-fatah
'akhbara `ani al-munhana wal-ghadeer
wal-lwża, wal-twlyba, hāta anà
tasier biya al-dunya itha ma 'asier
waqala ma qala, fla nijmatun
illa `alyiha min `abiry `abir
ghadan, yarani al-nasu fi sh`rihi
fama nabydhyan... wash`ran qasir
da`y hkayat al-nas, lan tusbihiy
kabirtan... ilà bihubi al-kabyer...
madha tasyer al-ardu law lam takun
law lam takun `aynaki.. madha tasyer?
        —*Nizar Qabbani (b.1923)*

A Brief Love Letter

My darling I have much to say
Where o precious one shall I begin?
All that is in you is princely
O you who makes of my words through their meaning
Cocoons of silk
These are my songs and this is me
This short book contains us
Tomorrow when I return its pages
A lamp will lament
A bed will sing
Its letters from longing will turn green
Its commas be on the verge of flight
Do not say why did this youth
Speak of me to the winding road and the stream
The almond tree and the tulip
So that the world escorts me wherever I go?
Why did he sing these songs?
Now there is no star
That is not perfumed with my fragrance
Tomorrow people will see me in his verse
A mouth the taste of wine, close-cropped hair
Ignore what people say
You will be great only through my great love
What would the world have been if we had not been
If your eyes had not been what would the world have been?
    —Nizar Qabbani (b.1923)
      Translated by Mounah Khouri & Hamid Algar

'Ila Qidysah

madha 'idhan tatawaq`in?
ya bid`atu 'imra'aha...'ajybi
ma 'aladhi tatawaq`in?
'a'adalu 'astad al-dhubab huna?
wa'anti tudakhinyn...
'ajtaru kalhashashu 'ahlami
wa'anti tudakhinyn...
wa'ana
'amamu saryruki al-zahy kaqit maskien
matat makhalibuhu wa'azthu...wahadathu al-sinyn
'ana lan 'akuwn_ ta'akadi
'al-qit al-ladhi tataswaryn...
qitan min al-khashab al-mujawaf la yuharikhu al-hanyn
yaghfu `ala al-kursi 'idh tatajaradien...
wayarudu `aynayahi...
'idha 'inhasarat qibab al-yasmien

tilka al-nihaya.. laysa tudhishni
famaliki tudhashien
hadha anā..
hadha al-ladhiy `indy..
famadha ta'murien?
'a`sabi 'ihtaraqat..
wa'anti `ala sariyriki taqra'ien
'a'asum 'an shafatayki?
fawqa rujulaty ma tatlubin..
ma hikmati?
ma tibati?
hadha ta`am al-maiytien..

mutasawaf
màn qala? 'ini 'ākhiru al-mutasawfien...
'ana lastu ya qidysati 'al-rabu al-ladhi tatakhyalien...
rajulun 'ana kalākharien...

♠

To a Saint

What then do you expect?
Tell me, o hunk of woman
What do you expect?
Shall I keep on chasing flies
While you smoke?
Chew on my dreams like a hashish addict
While you smoke?
And I in front of your resplendent bed
Am like a wretched cat
His claws and his honor dead
Destroyed by the years
Be sure I shan't be the cat you imagine
A hollow wooden cat unmoved by feeling
Dozing on the chair while you undress
Turning away his eyes
When the jasmine domes are revealed

That ending doesn't scare me
Why then are you scared?
This is me
This is what I have
What then are your orders?
My nerves are burnt up
And you lie reading on your bed
Must I vow a fast on your lips?
What you ask is too much for virility.
My wisdom?
My goodness?
Food for the dead!

A sufi!
Who said it? Me, the last of the sufis!
I am not, o "saint," the god whom you imagine
But a man like others

♠

bitharati...
binadhalati
rajulun 'anà kalākharien...
fihi maẓaya 'al-'anbiya'
wafihi kufru al-kafirien...
wwda`atu al-'atfal fihi.. waqwahu al-mutawahishien

rajulun 'ana kalàkharien
rajulun yuhibu _ 'idha 'ahibu
bikulu `unfu al-'arba`yn
láw kunti yawman tafhamien...
ma al-'arba`wn?
wama al-ladhi ya`niehi huba al-'arba`yn...
ya bid`atu 'imra'aha
láw 'anaki tafhamien...
                    —*Nizar Qabbani (b.1923)*

♠

In purity
And in vice
With the virtues of prophets
And the heresy of infidels
The gentleness of a child
And the cruelty of a savage

I am a man like others
A man who loves—when he does—
With all the violence of forty years
If only you understood
What that means, forty years
And what too the love of forty years
O hunk of women
If only you understood.

> —*Nizar Qabbani (b.1923)*
> *Translated by Mounah Khouri & Hamid Algar*

♠

Hiwar

"là taqul kana huby
khatiman 'aw siwar
'inā huby hisar
ināhu al-jamiwun
yubhirwuna 'ila mawtihum, yabhathwun...

là taqul kana huby
kamaran,
'inahu sharar."

—*Nizar Qabbani (b.1923)*

♠

Dialogue

Do not say my love was
A ring or a bracelet.
My love is a siege,
Is the daring and headstrong.
Who, searching sail out to their death.

Do not say my love was
A moon.
My love is a burst of sparks.
                    —*Nizar Qabbani (b.1923)*
                        Translated by Mounah Khouri & Hamid Algar

♠

Shykhukhah

shatawyatun 'ukhra
wahatha anà
huna...bejanbi al-madfa'a
'hlamu an tahlm biya 'imra'hatun
'hlamu an udfanu fi sadraha
siràn
fala taskhar min sriha
'hlamu an 'atluqa min munhana
`umry sinan
taqula: hatha al-sina
   mulki fala taqrub lahu 'imra'a

huna...bejanbi al-madfa'a
shatawyatun 'ukhra
wa-hatha ana
'ansju ahlami wa-'akhshaha
'akhfu àn taskharu 'aynaha
min sal`tu
hamqaù fi r'asiy
min shaybahtun
baydau an tarkul rijlaha
hubi...
fa'amsi anà
hunaka...janbu al-madfa'aha
el-`ubah talhu biha 'imra'aha
`ndi

wafi ghaden 'amutu min bardy
huna...bijanbi al-madfa'aha_
       — *Buland Al-Haidari (b.1926)*

86

♠

Old Age

Another winter,
And here am I,
By the side of the stove,
Dreaming that a woman might dream of me,
That I might bury in her breast
A secret she would not mock;
Dreaming that in my fading years
I might spring forth as light,
And she would say:
This light is mine;
Let no woman draw near it.

Here,
by the side of the stove,
Another winter,
and here am I,
Spinning my dreams and fearing them,
Afraid her eyes would mock
My bald, idiotic head,
My greying, aged soul,
afraid her feet would kick
My love,
And here, by the side of the stove,
I would be lightly mocked by woman.

Alone,
Without love, or dreams, or a woman,
And tomorrow I shall die of the cold within,
Here, by the side of the stove.
— *Buland Al-Haidari (b.1926)*
Translated by Mounah Khouri & Hamid Algar

♠

'Ihtiraq

wahta hiyna 'asharu jismaki al-hajary fi nariy
wa'anż` min yadayki al-thalj, tabqa bayna `aynayna
sahara min thulwj tunhik al-sary,
ka'anaki tanzuryn 'ilaya min sudumin wa'aqmar,
ka'ana, mundh kuna, fi 'intzar ma talaqayna.
walakena 'intzar 'al-huba luqya... 'ayna luqyana?
tamażaqa jismuki al-`ariy...
tamażaqa, tahta saqfi al-layl, nahduki bayna 'azfary...
tamażaqa kulu shay' min lahybi, ghayra 'astari
tahjibu fiki ma 'ahwah.
ka'any 'ashrab al-dama minki malhan, zala `atshanan
man 'istasqah. 'ayna hawaki? 'ayna fu'aduki al-`ary?
'asudu `alayki baba al-layl thuma 'u`anqu al-baba
fi'althumu fihi zily, dhikrayaty, ba`da 'asrariy...
wa'abhthu `anki fi nariy
fala 'alqaki, la 'alqa ramaiki fi al-luzah al-wary
sa'aqdhf kula nafsiy fi lizaha, kula ma ghaba
wama hadara.
'uryduki fi'uqtulyni kay 'uhisaki
  wa'uqtuly al-hajara
bifaydu damen, binarn minki...wa'ihtariqy bila nari!
          —*Bader Shaker 'Al-Sayab (1927-1964)*

♠

Burning

And even when I smelt your body of stone in my fire
And wrest the ice from your hands, between our eyes
Persist whole wastes of snow that devour the night-traveler
As if you saw me through mist and moonlight
As if we never met in hope and longing
Hope for love is a meeting...where then did we meet?
Your naked body is torn open
Your breasts, beneath the roof of night, are torn by my nails
My ardor has torn apart all but the veils
Which hide within what I desire
As if the blood I drink from you were salt
Whole draughts of it still not my thirst
Where is your passion? Where unbared heart?
I bolt on you the gate of night, then embrace the gate
Conceal within it my shadow, memories and secrets
Then search for you within my fire
And find you not, find not your ashes in the burning flame
I will cast myself into the flame, if it burns or not
Kill me, that I may feel you kill the stone
With a shedding of blood, with a spark of fire
...or burn then without fire.

     —*Bader Shaker 'Al-Sayab (1927-1964)*
     Translated by Mounah A. Khouri & Hamid Algar

Min al-`tabah ilá al-Samäu'

al-àn
walmatar al-hazien
yaghmurù wajhy al-hazien
ahlamu bsulamu min al-ghubar
min al-zhur al-mahdubah
walrahät al-madghutah `alá al-rukab
la's`du ilá a'aly al-samu'
wa'rifu
ayná tadhabu ahatuna wsalawatuna?
àh ya habibatiy
la buda ann takuna
kulu al-àhat wal-salawat
kulàh al-tanahudat wal-istighathat
al-muntaliqatu
min malàyeen al-afwahu wal-sudwru
w'brah àlaf al-sinyn wal-qurun
mutjam'ah fi makanin mah min al-samau'...kalghyum.
wlarubamah
kanat kalimati al-àn
kurba kalimat al-masyh
fà-linantazr al-samau'
ya habibatiy.

—*Muhammad al-Màghut (b.1930)*

From the Doorstep to Heaven

Now,
With the sad rain
Drenching my sad face,
I dream of a ladder of dust,
Collected from hunched backs
And hands clinging onto knees,
To mount to highest heaven
And discover
What becomes of our prayers and sighs.
O my beloved,
All the prayers and sighs,
All the laments and cries for help,
Springing from
Millions of lips and hearts,
Through thousands of years and centuries,
Must be gathered somewhere in heaven,
Like clouds.
And maybe
These words of mine
Are now close to those of Jesus.
So let us await the tears of heaven,
O beloved.

> —*Muhammad al-Màghut (b.1930)*
> *Translated by Mounah Khouri & Hamid Algar*

♠

Ilá `Aynayn `Gharybatien

sayidaty...
law lamasat `aynayki hadhy al-kalimatu al-`ashiqatu
sudfatan...law `abarat khilala al-shafatyn
fa`tadhiry `any li`aynayki
li'anany 'itaka'tu fi zilaha dhatu masa'
saraqtu ghafwah...
da`abt fi sukwnaha al-Nujwm wal-qamar
nasajat żwraqan kharafiyan, min waraq al-zahr
wasadatu rwhan mut`iban
saqieta shufah lahithah
'atfa'at shwqu `ayn

sayidaty...
hiyna il-taqiena sudfah liqa' al-ghuraba'
kanat ka'abaty mithly, tamshy fi al-tarieq
`ariyah bila qina`
masqwqah al-qadam...
kanat ka'abaty anti
wakan al-hużn, waldya`
kana al-samt, walnadam
yu`aniqan sha`iran 'anhakahu alsira`
walshi`ru ya sayidaty fi wataniy gharieb
yaktlhu al-faragh, wal-`adam
wa'intafadat rwuhy, hiyna absartuki ya sayidaty
sha`artu faj'ah, ka'ana khanjaran yaghwsu fi damy
yghsilu qalby, wafamy
yatrahany mukhadab al-jabien, dari`u al-yadayn
tahta zilali muqlatayki al-hlwatyn

sayidaty
law il-taqyna faj'ah...
law absarat `aynaya tilkum al-`aynyn
al-'ufqyn al-'khdaryn al-ghariqyn fi al-dabab wal-matar

♠

To Two Unknown Eyes

Mistress...
Should these enamored words chance to meet your eyes
Or pass between your lips
Then forgive me; it was your eyes
In whose shade one evening I leaned resting
And snatched brief slumber
In their repose I caressed the stars and moon
I wove a boat of fancy out of petals
And laid down my tired soul
Gave to drink my thirsty lip
Quenched my eye's desire

Mistress...
When we met by chance as strangers meet
My sorrow too was walking on the road
Bare, unveiled
With heavy tread
You were my sorrow
Sadness and loss
silence and regret
Were embracing a poet consumed by struggle
For poetry, mistress, is a stranger in my land
Killed by emptiness and void
My spirit trembled when I saw you
I felt suddenly as if a dagger delved into my blood
Cleansed my heart, my mouth
Prostrated me with soiled brow and supplicating hands
In the shade of your sweet eyes

Mistress...
If suddenly we meet
If my eyes see those your eyes
High-set, green, drowned in mist and rain

♠

law jama`tana sudfah 'ukhra `ala al-taryq
wakulu sudfah qadar
fasawfa 'althum al-taryq maratyn.
                    —*Muhammad al-Fayturi (b.1930)*

If on the road by another chance we meet
And what is chance but fate?
Then would I kiss the road, kiss it twice.
> —*Muhammad al-Fayturi (b.1930)*
> *Translated by Mouah A. Khouri & Hamid Algar*

♠

'Ahlam 'al-Faris al-Qadiem

law 'anana kuna kaghusnaiy shajarah
al-shamsu arda'at `urwqana ma`an
walfajru rawana nadan ma`an
thuma 'istbaghna khadratan muzdahirah
hiyna 'istatlna fa`tanaqna 'adhru`a
wafi al-rabiy`i naktasi thyabana al-mulawanah
wafi al-khariefi, nakhla`u al-thiyab, na`ara badana
wanastahimu fi al-shita, yudfi'una hunuwna
'aw 'anana kuna bishati al-bahri mawjatayn
sufiyata min al-rimal wal-mahar
tuwjata sabiekahtan min al-nahari wal-żabad
'aslamata 'al-`anan liltayar
yadfa`una min mahdana lilahdana ma`an
fi mashyaten raqisaten mudandanah
tashrabuna sahabatun raqieqah
tadhuwb tahta thaghri shamsin hulwahten raqieqah
thuma na`uwdu mawjatayn taw'amayn
'aslamata al-`anan lltayar
fi dawraten 'ila 'al-'abad
min al-bihari llsama'
min al-sama'i llbihari
law anana kuna bikhaymatyn jaratayn
min shurfaten wahidaten matla`una
fi ghaymatn wahidatn madja`una
nady'u ll`ushaqi wahdahum wallmusafiryn

nahwa diyari al-`ishqi wal-mahabah
wallhażana al-sahiryna al-hafizyna mawthiqa al-'ahibah
wahien ya'fulu al-żamanu ya habiybati
yudri kunna al-uwful
wayantafi gharamuna al-tawiylu bi'intifa'ina
yab`athuna al-'ilahu fi masaribi al-jinani duratayn
bayna hasan kathier

♠

Dreams of the Ancient Knight

If only we were the two boughs of a tree
The sun would nourish our roots together
And together, dawn would water us with dew
Then we would be tinted with blossoming verdure
When we grew long we would link our arms
In the spring don many-hued garments
In the autumn cast them off, baring our bodies
And bathe in the winter, warmed by our affection
If only we were two waves on the seashore
Pure of sand and shell
Crowned with an ingot of light and foam
Our reins grasped by the current
Driving us on together, from cradle to grave
With dancing, humming gait
A gentle cloud imbibes us.
And melts in the breath of a sweet and tender sun
Then again we are twin waves
Our reins grasped by the current
In an eternal cycle
From sea to sky
From sky to sea
If only we were two neighboring stars
Rising from the same lofty point
Setting behind the same cloud
Shedding light on solitary lovers and wayfarers
To the lands of love and passion
And on the wakeful sorrowers holding fast to their beloved's pact
When fortune sets, O my love
Decline will overtake us
Our long passion will be extinguished with us
God casting us along the streambeds of paradise like two pearls
 among pebbles

waqad yarana malakun 'idh ya`buru al-sabiel
fayanhani, hiyna nashudu 'aynahu 'ila safa'ina
yalqutna, yamsahna fi riesha, yu`jibhu bariquna
yarshuquna fi al-mafraqi al-tuhwr
law 'anana kuna janahay nawrasin raqieq
wana`imen, la yabrahu al-madiq
muhliqen `ala dhu'abati al-sufun
yubashr al-malah bilwsul
wayuqizu al-haniena ll'ahbabi walwatan
munqaruhu yaqtalu bilnasiem
wayartawi min `irqa al-ghuywm.

—Salah `Abd al-Sabur (b.1931)

♠

An angel might see us as he trod his path
And stoop down, his eye caught by our purity
Lift us up and rub us on his cloak, amazed at our luster
And then cast us back into the limpid crossroads.
If only we were the wings of a gentle, tender
Seagull, never leaving the strait
Hovering over the ship's wake
Giving the sailor tidings of arrival
Awakening desire for loved ones and for home
His beak nourished by the breeze
Drinking from the perspiration of the clouds.

—*Salah `Abd al-Sabur (b.1931)*
Translated by Mounah Khouri & Hamid Algar

♠

Maw`d

jam`un min al-nisa'i hwla rajulin muhatm
kultu bi'ibtisamah: nad`uhu qaysu laila
fahabatat al-hararhtu bisur`ah.

lam 'ara fi hayati `wyunan katilka al-mudhayalah
bilfasatien. wahyna traktuhu kana
lā buda lahuna ān yalhaqana biya
wa'intazrny hunaka 'imra'ahtan 'imra'aha.
kuntu fi madynah qarawyah, gharybahtu
al-'atwar, `ala difaf al-nahr. Wadwna
'ān 'abtasem. kana al-rajul al-muhatm qad 'at`abany.
watamā liqa'y bihuna fi al-bayt al-qadiem
fatahualat da`abaty ila dam.
waqatalatuhuna bilfaraghi al-klasiky.
                    —*Unsi al-Hājj (b. 1937)*

♠

Rendezvous

A group of women around a shattered man.
I said with a smile: Let's call him Qais, Laila's mad lover.
The temperature sank abruptly.

Never in my life did I see eyes like those with trailing dresses.
The moment I left him they had, of course, to come after me.
And there they waited for me, one after the other.
I was in a rural city, a strange place on the banks of the river.
And even without my smiling, the shattered man had tired me.
It was in the old house that our meeting took place, and my
    jokes turned into blood.
I killed them with classic boredom.

         —*Unsi al-Hājj (b. 1937)*
          Translated by Mounah A. Khouri & Hamid Algar

♠

Hiwar

quwli:
 bimadha tufakirin?
'ufakiru fi shamsika al-lati là tunirani yà `āshiqi.
quwli:
 bimadha tufakirin?
'ufakira fika, kayfa tastaty`a 'an tasbur `alà burwdahtu qalbi
quwli:
 bimadha tufakirin?
'ufakiru ya `ashiqi fi jabarwtika, kayfa 'anaka tuhibuni
wala 'uhibuka.

qul:
 bimadha tufakir?
'ufakir kayfa kunti, wa'hżan min 'ajliki ya habibati.
'ufakir fi shamsi l-lati 'adhabatki, wafi jaladi
al-ladhi khadda`aki,
'ufakir fi hubi al-ladhi rakka`aki, thuma mallaki ya habibati.
'ufakir fi l-marathi yà habibati.
'ufakir fi l-qatli.
                    —*Unsi al-Hājj (b. 1937)*

♠

Dialogue

I said:
Tell me, of what are you thinking?
—Of your sun which does not illuminate me, o beloved.
I said:
Tell me, of what are you thinking?
—Of you, and how you can endure the coldness of my heart.
I said:
Tell me, of what are you thinking?
—Of your might, o beloved, of how you can love me, when
                                        I do not love you.

She said:
Tell me, of what are you thinking?
—Of how you once were, and I grieve for you, o beloved.
I think too of my sun which melted you,
Of my patience which made you submit,
Of my love which brought you to your knees,
And then spurned you,
O beloved.
I think of elegies,
O beloved,
I think of murder.

> —*Unsi al-Hājj (b. 1937)*
> *Translated by Mounah A. Khouri & Hamid Algar*

♠

Ya Wajhaha

sha'a l-hawa 'an naltaqi...sahwan
kam kuntu 'aftaqiduk
ya wajhaha l-hilwu

kulu l-ladhi samaytuhu: shadwan
min qalbi ma 'ajidk;
'adha `alà shufahtu l-saba...laghwan

kun liya kama 'ahwa
'amtar `alaya l-dif'u wal-halwa
wayadaya tabuthu simatiki l-shajwah
fay'inu murta`idak

ya hinama 'a`iduki
'al-saiefu fiki yu`aniq al-sahwah
`aynaki tartakhiyan fi 'urjuhah
wal-thaghru murta`ishun bilà ma'wah
wa`adhabuhu: salwah
'in ji'tu 'anfudu `indahu l-shakwa

fi l-layli 'aftaqiduki
fatudi`u li qasamatuki l-nashwah
ta'ti khujuwlu l-bawhi mażhuwan
wa`alà dhira`u l-shawqi 'astaniduka
wa'hisu fi wajhi lada al-anfas
hina yalufani raghduki!
wa'anàm!
tahmilni rw'āki linijmah quswah
natarafq al-khutwah
nahki, fa'arshuf hamsuki l-rakhwah
wayahużuni sahwa...fa'aftaqiduki
lakin bila jadwah
bila jadwah!
ya wajhaha l-hulwah

♠

Oh...Her Face

Love wished us to meet...inadvertently
how I used to miss you
oh her pretty face.

All that I named: Chanted
from before I found you;
dawned on the lips of youth...foolish talk.

Be for me as I love
warmth and beauty rained on me
and my hands spread your elevated worries
and your fertile ground moaned.

Oh when I promise you
the summer in your embrace the awakening.
Your eyes get loose in a swing
and your mouth trembles with no shelter
and his torment: Consolation
if I came to shake his complaint.

At night I miss you
your intoxicated features light up to me
you come proudly shamed of disclosure
and I lean you against the arm of longing
and I feel in my face the blazing breaths
when your comfort wraps me!
and I sleep.
Seeing you carries me to a distant star
we step gently,
we talk, and I sip your loose whispers
that awaken me shaking...so I miss you
but with no use
with no use!

'amtar, fa'ini mujadab l-salwah
ma żiltu là 'aqwah
'an 'anqula l-khutwah
'in fatani sinduki

ya wajhaha al-hulwah
ma żiltu 'aftaqiduki
ma żiltu 'aftaqiduki
                    —'Amal Dunqul (1940-1982)

♠

Oh her pretty face
rains, as I am barren of consolation
I still don't have the strength
to move my steps
if I missed you leaning.

Oh her pretty face
I still miss you
I still miss you.

—'Amal Dunqul (1940-1982)
Translated by Farid Bitar

♠

al-'Aynan al-Khadrāwān

al-'aynan al-khadrāwān
marwahatàn
fi 'arwiqahtu l-saief al-haràn
'ughniyatan musafiratan
'abharata min nayāti l-ru`yan
bi`abiyr hanan
bi`aża' min ālihat al-nuwr 'ilà mudun l-'ahżan
sanatan
wa'ana 'abni żawraq hub
yamtad `alayhi min al-shawq shira`an
kai 'ubhir fi l-`aynayn l-safiyatyn
'ilà jużur l-murjan
ma 'hlā 'an ydtrub l-mawj fayansadil l-jafnan
wa'na 'abhath `an mijdaf
`an 'iman!

fi samt "al-katidra'iyat" l-wasnan
suwar "ll`adhra'"l-musabalah l-'ajfan
ya man 'arda`t l-hubu salaht l-ghufran
watamtah fi `aynayki l-musabalatyn
shababu l-hirman
ruddi jafnayki
la'ubsr fi `aynayki al-'alwan
'ahuma khadrawan
ka`uywni habibi?
ka`uywnin yubhiru fiha l-bahru bila shatān
yas'al `an hub
`an dhikra
`an nisyan!
qalbi harān, harān
wal-`aynan al-khadrawan
mirwahatān.

—'Amal Dunqul (1940-1982)

♠

The Green Eyes

The green eyes,
two propellers,
in the verandas of the hot summer.
Two traveling songs
sailed from the shepards' flutes
in a tender fragrance
with a consolation from the Gods of light to the cities of sadness.
Two years
and I have been building the boat of love.
Extends on it two sails of longing
so I can sail in the clear eyes
to the coral islands.
How sweet when the waves are unsettled so the eyelids drop
and I am searching for an oar for faith
in the silence of the splendoring cathedrals.

Pictures of the "virgin" with the lowered eyelids
you who breast-fed love of forgiveness prayer
and you mounted in your lowered eyes
the youth of deprivation.
Roll over your eyelids...
Are they green
like the eyes of my love?
Like eyes that the sea sails in with no shores
asking about love
about my memory
about forgetting?
My heart is heated, heated
and the green eyes
are propellers.

—'Amal Dunqul (1940-1982)
Translated by Farid Bitar

♠

Arabic Quotations & Proverbs

All proverbs and quotations translated by
Ghazi A. Algosaibi

♠

watalafatat `ayni famudh khafiyat
   `ani l-tulwlu talafata l-qalbu
                    —*Al-Shareef Al-Radhiy*

wa'asbahtu `aman lilfatahti mubajalan
   waqad kuntu 'ayama l-shababi laha 'akhan
                    —*Ibn Arrumi*

wa'ini lata`rwni lidhkraki hazatun
   kama 'intafada l-`asfwru ballahu l-qatru
                    —*Abu Sakhr Al-Huthli*

falyalu 'atwalu shay'in hiyana 'afqiduha
   walyalu 'aqsaru shay'in hiyna 'alqaha
                    —*Unknown*

laylati hadhihi `arwsun mina l-zunji
   `alayha qala'idun min juman
                    —*Al-Ma`arri*

'antani hawaha qabla 'an 'a`rif l-hawah
   fasadafa qalban khaliyan fatamakana
                    —*Ibn Attuthariyya*

walaysa l-buka ma tasfah l-`aynu 'inama
   'amarru l-buka 'ayni l-buka'u l-muwalaju
                    —*Ibn Arrumi*

sirrani fi khatiri l-zalma'a yaktumuna
   hatta yakada lisanu l-subhi yashfiyna
                    —*Ibn Zaydoun*

♠

My eyes turned back, the camp was no longer visible—
    my heart turned back.
                            —*Al-Shareef Al-Radhiy*

To the young maiden I became respected uncle;
    but in the days of youth I was a mate.
                            —*Ibn Arrumi*

When I think of you I tremble—
    a sparrow in the rain.
                            —*Abu Sakhr Al-Huthli*

The night is the longest thing when she is away,
    the shortest when she is around.
                            —*Unknown*

The evening is a black bride
    wearing silver necklaces.
                            —*Al-Ma`arri*

Her love arrived,
    found an empty heart and took possession.
                            —*Ibn Attuthariyya*

The most painful crying is not done through tears
    but from inside.
                            —*Ibn Arrumi*

She and I were like two secrets hidden by darkness
    and revealed by morning.
                            —*Ibn Zaydoun*

♠

`afah allahu `anha! hal abiytanna laylatan
  mina l-dahri là yasri 'ilaya khayaluha
                  —Tawba Ibn Alhimyar

laqad khiftu 'an 'alqa l-maniyatah faj'atan
  wafi l-nafsi hajātun 'ilayki kama hiya
                  —Jameel Ibn Ma`mar

khuliqtu 'al-wafan law raji`tu 'ila l-sibā
  lafaraqtu shaybi mawja`a l-qalbi bakiyā
                  —Al-Mutanabbi

nahnu qawmun tudhibuna l-'a`yuni l-nujlu
  `alà 'anana nudhibu l-hadida
                  —Abu Firas

ka`usfuratin fi kaffi tiflin yaswmuha
  warda hiyadi l-mawti watiflu yal`abu
                  —Qays Ibn Al-Mulawwah

idha mà 'ata yawmun yufarriqu baynana
  bimawtin fakun 'anta l-ladhi tata'akharu
                  —Al-Aqra` Ibn Habis

tatawala hatà kultu laysa bimunqadin
  walaysa l-ladhi yar`ah l-nujuma biāyibi
                  —Annabigha

wadadtu wabayti allahi 'anaki bikratun
  hijanun wa'ani mus`abun thuma nahrubu
                  —Kuthayyir

♠

God bless her,
    why does she visit every night in dreams?
                    —*Tawba Ibn Alhimyar*

How sad suddenly to die
    with all those unsatisfied longings for you.
                    —*Jameel Ibn Ma`mar*

My loyalty is such
    that I would return to youth broken-hearted.
                    —*Al-Mutanabbi*

We can melt steel
    but are easily melted by beautiful eyes.
                    —*Abu Firas*

I am like a sparrow in a boy's hand—
    the sparrow is dying but the boy plays on.
                    —*Qays Ibn Al-Mulawwah*

Were you and I to die in the same day,
    please be last.
                    —*Al-Aqra` Ibn Habis*

The night drags on,
    I think that dawn—the shepherd of the stars—will never return.
                    —*Annabigha*

Were you a she-camel
    I, a bull, and escape what bliss!
                    —*Kuthayyir*

♠

muwarradtun min kaffi dabiyn ka'anama
tanawalaha min khaddihi fa'adaraha
—Deek Al-Jinn

wa'inama 'awladuna baynana
'akbaduna tamshi `alà l-'ardi
—Hattan Ibn Al-Mu`alla

'ashwqan wlamma yamdi liya ghayru
fakayfa 'idha sara l-matiyyu bina `ashrah
—Abd Bani Al-Hashas

ka'ana l-ghamama laha `ashiqun
yusayiru hawdajaha haythu sarā
—Al-Ma`arri

'inna l-shababa `addtu l-tasabi
rawa'ihu l-jannati fi l-shababi
—Abu Al-Atahiya

nasibuka fi hayatika min habibin
nasibuka fi manamika min khayal
—Al-Mutanabbi

fa'in za`amta bi'anna l-huba ma`siyatun
falhubbu 'ahsanu mà yu`sa bihi allahu
—Al-Abbas Ibn Al-Ahnaf

'ajaratna 'inna ghariebani hahuna
wakulu ghariebin lilghariebi nasiebu
—Umru'u Al-Qays

♠

She served rose-like wine
   from the vineyards in her cheeks.
                        —*Deek Al-Jinn*

Our children are our hearts
   developing feet and walking.
                   —*Hattan Ibn Al-Mu`alla*

Such yearning on the caravan's first night—
   what about the tenth?
                   —*Abd Bani Al-Hashas*

Clouds are in love with her,
   they follow her caravan everywhere.
                   —*Al-Ma`arri*

Youth is fun
   Youth is the perfume of paradise.
                   —*Abu Al-Atahiya*

Can you hang on to beloved ones?
   Can a sleeper hang on to dreams?
                   —*Al-Mutanabbi*

You say love is a sin?
   I say love is God's favorite sin!
                   —*Al-Abbas Ibn Al-Ahnaf*

Here we are both strangers;
   strangers are relatives.
                   —*Umru'u Al-Qays*

♠

lana l-jafanatu yalma`na fi l-duha
  wa'asyafuna yaqturna min najdah damā
                    —*Hassan Ibn Thabit*

'alà layta l-shababa ya`wdu yawman
  fa'akhbirhu bima fa`ala l-mashiebu
                    —*Huthbah Ibn Khashram*

tashtāqu 'ayyara nufusu l-warah
  wa'innama l-shawqu 'ilà wardihi
                    —*Al-Ma`arri*

wayalayta 'anna allaha 'in lam 'ulàqiha
  qada bayna kullu 'ithnayn 'allà talaqaya
                    —*Hafs Alaleemy*

'udhkwruna mithla dhikrana lakum
  rubba dhikra qarrabat min nazha
                    —*Mihyar*

wadhawu l-shawqi l-qadiemi wa'in ta`azza
  mashuwqun hiyna yalqa l-`āshiqina
                    —*Omar Ibn Abi Rabi`a*

lahaki allahu yà dunyan khulwban
  fa'anti l-ghadatu l-bikru l-`ajuwzu
                    —*Al-Ma`arri*

abati l-rrawadifu wal-thudiyyu liqamsiha
  massa l-butwni wa'an tamasa zuhurā
                    —*Unknown*

♠

These are our silver pots glowing, inviting guests,
    and those are our swords dripping with blood.
                —Hassan Ibn Thabit

Youth! Please return.
    I have so many tales to tell you about old age.
                —Huthbah Ibn Khashram

It is not May but the roses of May
    that people love.

                —Al-Ma`arri

If I am not to meet her,
    may no lovers ever meet!
                —Hafs Alaleemy

Think of us!
    such thoughts bridge distances.
                —Mihyar

Old lovers forget old romances
    until they meet young lovers.
                —Omar Ibn Abi Rabi`a

Life be damned!
    you pretty, ancient virgin.
                —Al-Ma`arri

The dress cannot touch her waist, thanks to her breast;
    or her back, thanks to her buttocks.
                —Unknown

♠

ghaydana min `abaratihinna waqulna liya:
  madha laqieta min l-hawah walaqiena
—Jareer

faqalat: laqad 'azra bika l-dahru ba`dana
  faqultu: ma`adha 'allahi bal 'anti là l-dahru
—Abu Firas

lam abki 'atlālika lakinnama
  bakaytu `ayshi fika 'idh wallà
—Unknown

qarrabatha l-muna waba`adaha l-na'iyu
  fa'adhat minni ba`idan qarieba
—Abu Tammam

fawadadtu taqbila l-suywfi li'annaha
  lama`at kabariqi thaghriki l-mutabassimi
—Antara

wa'sbahtu min layla l-ghadata kaqabidin
  `alà l-mā'i khanathu furwju l-'asabi`i
—Qays Ibn Thurayh

qultu labayki 'idh da`ani laki l-shawqu
  wallhadiyyni karrah l-matiyya
—Qays Ibn Al-Mulawwah

tarjuw ghadan waghadun kahamilatin
  fi l-hayyi là yadruwna mà talidu
—Bashar

♠

Drying their tears they asked:
  "So this is what love is all about?"
                                —*Jareer*

"Life has been unkind to you" she said;
  "thou; not life" I replied.
                                —*Abu Firas*

It is not the ruins I mourn
  but my sweet memories.
                                —*Unknown*

Dreams bring her close, distances take her away;
  she is the close-distant one.
                                —*Abu Tammam*

I felt like kissing the swords
  because their glimmer reminded me of your smile.
                                —*Antara*

Layla is gone—
  water seeping through clenched fingers.
                                —*Qays Ibn Thurayh*

Love called,
  I turned back the caravan and hurried to you.
                                —*Qays Ibn Al-Mulawwah*

Tomorrow is a pregnant woman
  bearing an unknown baby.
                                —*Bashar*

♠

'anà fardu l-hawah kama 'anta fardu
l-husni mustakbirun `an l-'andadi
—*Ibn Arrumi*

kunna ka'anjumi laylin baynaha qamarun
yajlw l-dujah fahawah min bayniha l-qamaru
—*Safeyya Al-Bahiliyya*

fa'in tamna`w layla watahmw biladaha
`alayya falan tahmw `alayya l-qawafiya
—*Qays Ibn Al-Mulawwah*

ya bani āadamin! ta`ālw nunadi
'inama nahnu llnisa'i `abidu
—*Al-Abbas Ibn Al-Ahnaf*

'inna llahi fi l-`ibadi manaya
sallatatha `alà l-qulwbi l-`uyuwnu
—*Abu Tammam*

'idha 'ishtabakat dumw`un fi khudwdin
tabayyana man bakah miman tabakah
—*Al-Mutanabbi*

qalw l-rahilu fama shakaktu bi'anaha
ruwhi `an l-ddunya turidu rahilà
—*Abu Tammam*

♠

We are both made unique—
   I, by love, You by beauty.
                        —*Ibn Arrumi*

He was the moon, we were stars;
   the moon was struck down, the night is dark.
                    —*Safeyya Al-Bahiliyya*

You can stop me from visiting Layla,
   but how can you stop my lyrics?
                    —*Qays Ibn Al-Mulawwah*

Sons of Adam!
   let us together proclaim we are slaves of women.
                    —*Al-Abbas Ibn Al-Ahnaf*

Deaths of lovers are decreed through beautiful eyes.
                    —*Abu Tammam*

Real tears distinguish real lovers from fakes.
                    —*Al-Mutanabbi*

"Farewell," they said,
   "Farewell" whispered my soul to the world.
                    —*Abu Tammam*

♠

'awahi 'in nazarat wa'in hiya 'a`radat
   waq`u al-sihami wanaż`uhuna 'aliem
               —*Ibn Alrrumi*

fama labisa al-`ushāqu min khulal al-hawah
   walà khala`wu 'ilà al-thiyaba al-lati 'ablā
         — `*Ashriqa al-Moharibiyah*

'u`aniquha wal-nafsu ba`du mashuwaqatun
   'ilayha wahal ba`da al-`inaqi tadani
               —*Ibn Alrrumi*

billahi ya zabyati al-qa`i qulna lana
   layali minkunna 'am laila mina al-bashari
               —*Al-'Arji*

`indi rasa'ilu shawqin là 'abuwhu biha
   lawlà al-`adhwlu laqad balaghtuha faki
             —*Al-Shareef Al-Radhiy*

hawaha hawan lam ya`rifi al-qalbu ghayrahu
   falaysa lahu qablun walaysa lahu ba`du
             —*Al-Abbas Ibn Al-Ahnaf*

'ana wallahi 'ashtahi sihra `aynayki
   wa'khsha masari`a al-`ushaqi
             —*Bashar*

♠

She looks, the arrow penetrates.
  She turns away, the arrow is pulled out.
                              —Ibn Alrrumi

All those pretty dresses of love that lovers put on and take off
  are my castaways.
                     —`Ashriqa al-Moharibiyah

I embrace her,
  yet I still long for intimacy.
                              —Ibn Alrrumi

Gazelles of the valley, please tell me—
  is Layla one of you? or is she a woman?
                              —Al-`Arji

I have love messages waiting to be delivered
  directly to your mouth.
                     —Al-Shareef Al-Radhiy

Her love in my heart:
  nothing before, nothing after.
                     —Al-Abbas Ibn Al-Ahnaf

By God! I am fond of your eyes
  but fearful of death-traps within.
                              —Bashar

♠

'ina al-muhibyna qawmun bayna 'a`yunihum
    wasamun min al-hubi là yakhfa `alà 'ahad
                —Al-`Abbas Ibn-'Ahnaf

laqad kashafa al-'ithra'u minka khala'qan
    mina al-luw'mi kanat tahta thawbn min al-faqri
                —'Abu Al-Haul

khala minki tarfi wa'mtalā minki khatiri
    ka'anaki min `ayni nuqilti 'ilà qalbi
                —'Al-Abbas Ibn 'Alhnaf

'uhibuka hubayni huba al-hawah
    wahuban li'anaka 'ahlun lidhaka
                —Rabi`a Al-`Adawiyya

żawidyna min husni wajhiki mà dāma
    fa-husnu al-wujuhi halun tahulu
                —Al-Mutanabbi

wama al-nasu 'ilà al-`ashiquwna dhawwu al-hawa
    walà khyra fi man la yuhibu waya`shaqu
                —'Al-Abbas Ibn `Alhnaf

al-mā'u fi naziri wal-naru fi kabidi
    'in shi'ti faghtarifi 'aw shi'ti fa'iqtabisi
                —Al-Shareef Al-Radhiy

♠

Humans are those capable of love,
    Others are useless!
                        —`Al-`Abbas Ibn-`Ahnaf

Wealth has revealed in you
    an evil spirit hidden by poverty.
                        —Abu Al-Haul

You departed from my sight and entered my thoughts,
    traveled from my eyes to my heart.
                        —`Al-Abbas Ibn `Alhnaf

I love you twice: because I am so passionate,
    because you are so perfect.
                        —Rabi`a Al-`Adawiyya

Let us enjoy the beauty of your face—
    such a beauty is short-lived.
                        —Al-Mutanabbi

Lovers carry between their eyes
    a mark of love nobody misses.
                        —`Al-Abbas Ibn `Alhnaf

There is water in my eyes and fire in my heart
    do you want a drink or a spark?
                        —Al-Shareef Al-Radhiy